THE COOKBOOK

# west

RESTAURANT

*Cook with thought!*
*Best Wishes*

WARREN GERAGHTY

with contributions from
DAVID HAWKSWORTH,
RHONDA VIANI,
DAVID WOLOWIDNYK,
OWEN KNOWLTON

text by JIM TOBLER

photography by JOHN SHERLOCK

# THE COOKBOOK
## west
### RESTAURANT

DOUGLAS & MCINTYRE
Vancouver / Toronto / Berkeley

Douglas & McIntyre Ltd.
2323 Quebec Street, Suite 201
Vancouver, British Columbia
Canada v5t 4s7
www.douglas-mcintyre.com

*Library and Archives Canada Cataloguing in Publication*
Geraghty, Warren
West : the cookbook / Warren Geraghty.
Includes index.
ISBN 978-1-55365-357-8
1. Cookery, Canadian—British Columbia style.
2. Cookery—British Columbia—Vancouver.  3. West (Restaurant).  I. Title.
TX714.G465 2008    641.509711′33    C2008-903093-1

Jacket and text design by Jessica Sullivan
Jacket photographs by John Sherlock
Photos by John Sherlock
Printed and bound in Canada by Friesens
Printed on acid-free paper
Distributed in the U.S. by Publishers Group West

We gratefully acknowledge the financial support of the Canada Council for the
Arts, the British Columbia Arts Council, the Province of British Columbia through
the Book Publishing Tax Credit, and the Government of Canada through the
Book Publishing Industry Development Program (BPIDP) for our publishing activities.

# contents

# dining out west

Vancouver's iconic Granville Street, which leads north to a breathtaking cityscape against a backdrop of mountains, is a bustling thoroughfare home to unique boutiques, theatres and eateries that reflect the rich history and diversity of the West Coast's terminal city. Nestled within this tapestry, at 13th Avenue, is West, a restaurant that has embraced the bounty of the city and the surrounding region. Driven by the guiding philosophy of providing each guest with the freshest, most flavourful food experience, West has developed an international reputation as a leader in fine dining.

West today is not the place it was when it opened, although a coherent personality has seen it evolve from the beginning. Brian Hopkins is the restaurant director. He was with the restaurant on day one, when the name was Ouest, and says now, "I always believed in this restaurant. We had growing pains, but I knew this was a great place and a great idea for this region." Owner Jack Evrensel, already an experienced restaurateur as the owner of Whistler's Araxi and Vancouver's CinCin, was in the process of opening another restaurant in Vancouver, the Blue Water Cafe + Raw Bar, when the space on Granville Street

became available. An industry veteran proclaimed that no one had opened two fine-dining establishments simultaneously and that it could not be done, but Jack felt prepared to face the challenge. Jack says, "At first we simply wanted to bring something special to Vancouver. At the same time, as with our other restaurants, I didn't want people to say, 'Great restaurant—at least for Vancouver standards.' The idea has always been to create great restaurants that would work in any major city."

Brian recalls the first evening's service at Ouest, the Granville restaurant, from the menu, complete with rabbit and oxtail, to the way the servers presented the dishes in high French formal style—plates arriving on trays, often under silver covers, unveiled simultaneously to every diner at the table. Ouest tapped into a clientele of curious and genuinely passionate folks who were hungry for just such a dining room in this city.

The first incarnation of the room featured a high ceiling, a completely frosted glass window at front, and a wall that kept the bar and entryway completely separate from the main dining room. Ouest had a loyal following from the outset, but as time went on, the key staff—including Jack himself—perceived that the restaurant was not quite the gem it was intended to be. Jack says, simply, "It wasn't connecting." After thinking, considering options and debating with the architect, manager and chef, Jack encountered divided opinions on what to do. The decision to transform Ouest, the French dining experience, to West, the Pacific Coast fine-dining experience, focussing on local and seasonal ingredients prepared with imagination, was not an easy one to make, but Jack felt that this restaurant should directly take into account the neighbourhood, city and region of which it is a part.

Today, when guests walk into West, they're greeted on the right with the bar, backed by a wall of wine in wooden bins. A four-foot partition separates the bar from the main dining room, which boasts a large, mural-size mirror on its south wall. These design features lend an expansiveness to an intimate space that allows diners to define their own experience at West, whether they wish to take in the seemingly ceaseless activity at the bar or focus on the food and the company at the table.

Designer Werner Forster, who when he passed away left an impressive architectural and design legacy of private homes and restaurants, was passionate about details—he spent a lot of time contemplating a project before setting formal pen to draft design paper. His step daughter, Sandy Sengara, says, "West is such a compact space, and Werner thought of it as his most classical work. He enjoyed those great, long meetings at the bar, discussing what the changes might be and should be. And then he would go out and visit other restaurants and doodle." Werner Forster knew his own mind and was not one to brook others' opinions in any haphazard way, but he was also a professional who thoughtfully considered his clients' needs. He shaped the space with a slightly more relaxed, personable approach, making it warmer while maintaining its fundamental elegance. The room was, as Jack states, "completely re-energized." The more open, fresh room and the restaurant's lighter-touch service appealed to established clients and also attracted a whole new clientele that found the space more welcoming.

Brian puts it well: "Today, we have our international guests, which we've always had, and we have dedicated regulars, foodies and non-foodies. But what I really like is that now there are people who live in this area who are thrilled to be able to just walk down the hill and have food of this quality."

spring

# chef warren geraghty on the road less travelled

The paths people take to a particular place in the food industry are seemingly tortuous if compared with the trajectory of other types of careers. But in the world of fine dining, working in a multitude of establishments is really the best way for a talented, ambitious young chef to develop the skills necessary to perform at a high level and to arrive as executive chef in a great restaurant. Warren Geraghty, executive chef at West since February 2008, wholeheartedly embraced this lifestyle as he made his way through the fine-dining scene in London, with some significant forays into France thrown in. He says that his journey allowed him to learn "a wide range of styles and techniques, from the classical, at Chez Nico and Orrery, to the more modern styles of The Halkin, Pied à Terre and Neat."

Warren tells the story of his beginnings in the industry: "Starting from the very bottom of the ladder, when I was fourteen years old, I worked my way up, slowly and surely, learning butchery, fishmongery, bakery, and so on, so that today I can apply all these skills in the kitchen." Fourteen is a tender age, and at that point in his life, Warren was reasonably certain he would follow his father and his grandfather into

the Army. But cooking in a local restaurant for two years convinced him that going to catering college might be a good idea. After being named student chef of the year, he decided to leave home and really pursue his cooking career. Warren disarmingly says, "I saw an advert for a commis position at a restaurant called Chez Nico. I applied not realizing this was one of perhaps the top five places in all of England at that time. I accepted the job, offered by a portly old chef, who of course was Nico himself; I had entered the world of Michelin dining without even knowing it."

Warren had the desire and the work ethic to survive a trial by fire. Through his work with Nico, he developed a skein of connections throughout the London food scene, which was just beginning to give France a run for its money.

Having trained with Richard Neat at Pied à Terre in London, Warren took the opportunity to further his learning and experience by accompanying Neat to Cannes to open a new restaurant there. Neat had trained under the "Godfather of French cooking," Joel Robuchon. In Cannes, Neat became the first non-French chef since the end of World War II to earn a Michelin star in France, a fact that ruffled some feathers in the French food establishment. "It was an interesting time," says Warren. "We were very popular before being awarded the star, but afterwards, well, it was like we were being punished for being so successful." Neat left after one year, and Warren became executive chef, maintaining the star to the day he returned to London.

Through such a training path, Warren understood the importance of developing his own sense of style, even as the luminaries he worked under drummed technique and methodology into him. "I think we as chefs all strive to develop our own identity, although we always carry with us the influences of our teachers and role models. The amalgamation of all these actually creates a new style almost by themselves. And taking over from another chef is an important part of that. You cannot upset the flow and pattern that exists, and you want to tap into the passion, skills and dedication of the team."

Warren, through his experiences, has accumulated his share of stories, and they always revolve around the ingredients that make their way to the plate: "Stefano Cavallini (a famous Italian chef in London who came from Milan's Ristorante Gualtiero Marchesi) and I were invited to the annual truffle auction in Alba. The auction was held in a castle on top of a huge hill in Alba. We were seated amongst some of Europe's top chefs as well as football players and other celebrities. There was a live video link to Las Vegas and New York, with each truffle being bid on at all three locations. It slowly builds up to the largest truffle of the evening (I don't remember exactly, but it was something like 800 g), which went for a huge sum I believe to Wolfgang Puck. After the auction we were all gathered in a massive dining room where we were served a wonderful seven-course dinner all accompanied by generous amounts of white truffle.

"The next morning we ventured out into the Piedmont countryside in our rental car, until we reached a small vineyard owned by a friend of Stefano's. After a couple of phone calls we were ushered into a truck and driven into the forest where we met an old gentleman who was introduced to us as one of the best truffle hunters in Piedmont. We were led round in circles to confuse us as to our location. The areas that these men hunt in are fiercely protected, as are the dogs; a good one can be worth thousands, and it is not uncommon for a dog to be killed by a rival hunter. After a polite but very quick tour of his hunting lodge we were ushered into a small room to do business.

"The truffles were laid out on a cloth on the table, a state-of-the-art scale was produced, and we decided to purchase a kilo. The price quoted was 3,000 euros per kilo. The weighing was done in full view of everyone, and the total was 1,012 g. I swiftly handed over 3,000 euros, but then I realized the loud remonstrations coming from the hunter meant that he wanted payment for the

12 g as well. So, after fishing through our pockets we coughed up the remainder and were ushered out and on another confusing wander through the woods."

Warren's route to the truffles—meandering but ultimately rewarding—serves as an apt metaphor for his career path: commis chef, Berystede Hotel; chef de partie, Chez Nico (Michelin 3 stars); chef de partie, Pied à Terre (2 stars); senior chef de partie, Stefano Cavallini at The Halkin (1 star); junior sous chef, The Orrery (1 star); junior sous chef, The Greenhouse; sous chef, then head chef, Restaurant Neat, Cannes (1 star); head chef, Aurora; executive sous chef, Four Seasons Hotel Hampshire; head chef, then executive chef, L'Escargot (1 star). And then West.

"I met Jack, saw his enthusiasm and recognized his dedication to only the top-quality ingredients. I also like the way he motivates and encourages people," says Warren. "I think the people at West are dedicated to the same things I am: offering fresh, flavourful food in surroundings that make guests feel comfortable and relaxed while still giving them the feeling of being waited on, taken care of, with grace and manners. I also love being part of a team, teaching and learning from each member of the brigade." The new era at West began February 2008. It is not the first, nor will it likely be the last, but one thing is certain: it is exciting and inventive, and it offers a new perspective in cooking for the region.

# salad of marinated calamari
# and sweet peppers with wild greens

CALAMARI SALAD

½ oz cilantro, chopped
(about 2 Tbsp)

1 small red chili, chopped

Juice of 1 small orange

1½ Tbsp white wine vinegar

1 cup olive oil

2 squids, 8 oz each, cleaned
and tentacles removed

1 red bell pepper

1 yellow bell pepper

6 oz wild salad greens
(about 4 cups)

*Serves 4*

This salad works well with any mixture of wild salad greens. Try a simple combination of wild arugula and frisée or a more elaborate mix of diverse leaves such as sorrel, kale, young cress shoots and edible flowers. This recipe marries the Mediterranean flavours of roasted pepper and hummus. Any leftover hummus can be stored in an airtight container in the refrigerator and used as a dip or a spread.

CALAMARI SALAD  In a medium bowl, combine cilantro, chili, orange juice, vinegar and ¾ cup of the olive oil, then season with salt and pepper and whisk together to make a marinade.

Slit each squid tube along its length to form one flat sheet of flesh. Score the squid gently on the inside in a criss-cross pattern.

Preheat a grill pan on high heat. Brush squid tubes with 3 Tbsp of the olive oil, season with salt and pepper, then place on the grill for 2 minutes each side. Remove the squid from heat and cut each tube into twelve to fifteen irregular triangles and place them into the marinade.

Preheat the oven to 350°F.

Heat the remaining 1 Tbsp of olive oil in a medium, ovenproof sauté pan on high heat. Add whole bell peppers and turn them in the pan for 2 minutes,

HUMMUS

9 oz cooked chickpeas
(about 2 cups)

2 cloves garlic, chopped

3 Tbsp olive oil

4 tsp fat-free Greek yogurt

1 tsp tahini

then place the pan into the oven for 15 minutes. Remove the peppers from the oven, place them into a bowl and cover the bowl with plastic wrap. After 15 minutes, remove the skin and seeds from the peppers and cut the peppers into irregular triangles about the same size as the squid pieces. Add to the marinade with the squid.

HUMMUS  Place chickpeas, garlic, olive oil, yogurt and tahini into a blender. Blend until smooth and pass the hummus through a sieve to get rid of any lumps. Season to taste with salt.

TO SERVE  On each of four plates, spread about 2 tsp of hummus in a ring on the plate. Top the hummus ring with a quarter of the squid and peppers. In a small bowl, toss the wild greens with about 2 Tbsp of the marinade, then heap a quarter of the greens in the centre of each plate.

SUGGESTED WINE  Great wines to pair with bitter greens and calamari that are also easy on the wallet are vinho verde from northern Portugal or an albariño from Rias Baixas. With their softly perfumed nose and crisp acidity they make very interesting food wines but will not steal the show. Be sure to drink them when they're fresh, fruity and youthful.

# tian of skate and crab with chilled cucumber and mint velouté

16 cups court bouillon (page 229)

1 Dungeness crab, about 2 lbs

4 tsp mayonnaise (page 239)

Juice of ½ lemon

1 oz fresh chives,
finely chopped (about 1 Tbsp)

1 wing of skate, 1 lb

2 Tbsp olive oil

2 Tbsp unsalted butter

1 English cucumber,
quartered, seeded and sliced
into thin ribbons on a mandolin
but with trimmings reserved

½ oz onion, finely chopped
(about 1 heaping Tbsp)

½ oz fresh mint

Deep-fried parsley
for garnish (page 237)

*Serves 4*

Skate is a kite-shaped fish also known as a ray and is related to sharks. The dense, meaty texture of the skate contrasts well with the flaky consistency of the crab in this dish.

In a large pot, bring court bouillon to a boil. Add crab and cook for 12 minutes, then remove the pot from heat and allow the crab to cool in the bouillon. Reserve the boullion. Pick the crab meat from the shell: first, twist off the legs and claws and set them aside. To remove the back, hold the base of the crab with one hand and pull the shell away from the body with the other hand. Discard the soft gills and the intestine, which runs down the centre of the back. Spoon out the soft brown meat, also known as crab butter or viscera, and reserve. Gently rinse the crab shell and crack it into four pieces—doing this will allow you easier access to the white meat in the corners of the shell. Pick out all of the crab's white meat—from the legs, claws and rest of the body. Set aside four leg pieces for the garnish.

Pass the brown meat through a fine sieve into a small bowl and fold in 2 tsp of the mayonnaise. Season with salt and pepper and half of the lemon juice. In another small bowl, combine the white meat, the remaining 2 tsp of mayonnaise and chives. Season with salt and pepper and the rest of the lemon juice. Refrigerate both bowls of crab meat.

Preheat the oven to 350°F.

Season the skate wing with salt and pepper. Heat a non-stick sauté pan on high heat. Add 1 Tbsp of the olive oil, then place the skate wing in the pan and sear for 1 minute. Add butter and allow it to brown, about 3 minutes, *Recipe continued overleaf. . .*

then turn the skate wing over and roast in the oven until it is cooked through, 8 to 9 minutes. Remove the skate wing from the pan and place it on a cutting board. Remove the flesh from the cartilage with a thin, sharp knife.

Grease a piece of parchment paper cut to 14 inches × 8 inches. Lay the skate wing, roasted side down, on the parchment to form a rectangle about 12 inches × 4 inches. Spoon the white crab meat mixture lengthwise down the centre, then fold the sides of the skate over the crab, tucking in the ends to form a roll. Wrap the roll first in aluminum foil to preserve the shape, then in plastic wrap to hold it. Refrigerate for at least 3 hours.

Finely cut the cucumber trimmings. In a medium sauté pan, heat the remaining 1 Tbsp of olive oil on medium heat. Add onion and sweat until translucent, about 2 minutes. Add cucumber trimmings and enough court bouillon to half cover, about ½ cup. Cook for 3 to 4 minutes. Pour this mixture into a blender, add mint and blend until smooth. Pass this velouté through a sieve and season with salt and pepper. Chill over ice.

TO SERVE  Slice the skate roll into four 3-inch tians. Spread the brown meat mixture over the side of each piece, then wrap the tian in cucumber ribbons. In each of four bowls, place one cucumber-wrapped tian. Garnish with the crab leg meat and fried parsley. Ladle a quarter of the velouté around the tian and serve.

SUGGESTED WINE  A dry, aromatic white is the way to go with the rich crab and skate in this dish. Try a dry muscat from B.C.; its pit-fruit and orange-blossom character also makes an interesting combination with the ethereal mint and cucumber velouté. A dry Alsatian gewürztraminer or muscat would also be a good choice.

NEAR THE WASHINGTON STATE fishing village of Dungeness is the site of the first *Cancer magister* commercial fishery, which was established well over a century ago. The Dungeness crab, as we commonly know it, is fished all the way from California's Bodega and Half Moon bays to Alaska's Aleutian Islands. It is one of thirty-five crab species found in British Columbia's coastal waters, and 224 licenced vessels bring in an average of three thousand tons per annual commercial catch. Only males with a shell width of at least six and a half inches can be brought to market. These crabs would be about four or five years old—an optimal age for food purposes, since they would have gained roughly 20 per cent body weight in each of approximately twelve moults, becoming fully grown. They would therefore expend their energy less on simple weight gain and more on body development, a fact that means more of that treasured, sweet meat.

Queen Charlotte Sound has a later breeding and moulting season than areas farther south and inland, and it is here that Lobster Man concentrates its fishery for the fresh crabs that begin to arrive at West in very early spring. Although the time-honoured way to serve this succulent meat is freshly boiled with a little pot of drawn butter alongside for dipping, the chefs at West are always innovating new ways to explore the crab's delicate flavour and texture. Since they use the freshest Dungeness crabs available anywhere, from some of the most pristine and frigid waters of the entire Pacific coastline, the spring menu at West serves as a fittingly celebratory tribute to this chief crustacean of the west.

dungeness crab

# tortellini of dungeness crab with cauliflower purée, pickled florets and light crab bisque

16 cups court bouillon (page 229)

1 Dungeness crab, about 2 lbs

2 Tbsp olive oil

¼ onion, finely diced

1 rib celery, finely diced

¼ head fennel, finely diced

1 clove garlic, finely diced

1 tsp tomato paste

2 Tbsp brandy

2 sprigs tarragon

⅓ cup whipping cream

8 oz pasta dough (page 237)

4 oz chicken mousse (page 233)

½ oz chives, chopped (about 1 Tbsp)

Deep fried parsley
for garnish (page 237)

*Serves 4*

CRAB TORTELLINI AND BISQUE   In a large pot, bring court bouillon to a boil. Add crab and cook for 12 minutes. Remove from heat and allow the crab to cool in the bouillon. Pick the crab meat from the shell: first, twist off the legs and claws and set them aside. To remove the back, hold the base of the crab with one hand and pull the shell away from the body with the other hand. Discard the soft gills and the intestine. Spoon out the soft brown meat and reserve it for other recipes. Gently rinse the crab shell and crack it into four pieces. Pick out all of the crab's white meat—from the legs, claws and rest of the body—and set this meat aside in the refrigerator. Break crab shells into 2-inch pieces.

In a large, heavy-bottomed pan, heat olive oil on medium heat. Add onion, celery, fennel and garlic and roast for 6 minutes. Add crab shells and tomato paste and roast for another 5 minutes. Add brandy, then ignite with a flame to flambé. After the flame has died, cover the mixture with cold water. Bring to a boil, then reduce heat, cook for 40 minutes and add tarragon. Strain the liquid through a sieve into another pot, and discard the solids. Bring the liquid to a boil and heat for 10 to 12 minutes until reduced by half, skimming any impurities off the surface during the process. Add cream and season this bisque with salt and pepper.

Roll pasta to the thickness of a dime. Cut twelve 2½-inch-diameter rounds.

Mix crab meat with chicken mousse and chives, then season the mixture with salt and pepper. Place 2 tsp of the crab mixture in the centre of a round of pasta. Moisten the edges and fold the pasta over the filling to make a tortellino, pinching the edges to seal. Repeat with the remaining pasta rounds. *Recipe continued overleaf. . .*

1 head cauliflower, about 8 oz,
cut into florets but stalk
and trimmings reserved

1 cup pickling liquor (page 239)

2 tsp unsalted butter

⅓ cup 2% milk

⅓ cup chicken stock (page 231)

PURÉE AND FLORETS  Heat a medium pot of water to a boil. Add cauliflower florets and blanch for 2 minutes. Remove the florets from the water, combine them with the pickling liquor in a medium non-reactive bowl and set aside.

Finely cut the cauliflower stalks and trimmings. In a small sauté pan, heat butter on high heat, then add the stalks and sweat for 1 minute. Cover with milk and chicken stock and cook until soft, about 10 minutes. Purée this mixture in a blender, season with salt and pepper and pass through a fine sieve.

TO SERVE  Bring a large pot of salted water to a boil. Add tortellini and cook for 5 minutes. Drain the pasta, then season with salt and pepper. Warm the cauliflower purée and crab bisque and remove the cauliflower florets from the pickling liquor.

In each of four bowls, spoon a quarter of the purée. Top with three tortellini and a quarter of the florets. Whisk the bisque vigorously, then ladle it into the bowls and garnish with fried parsley.

SUGGESTED WINE  A ripe, medium-bodied white wine like New World viognier from California or Australia would match the rich sweetness of the Dungeness crab and the flavour-packed bisque. If you prefer a more lively acidity in your whites, try the pungent zesty citrus fruit flavours of Marlborough sauvignon blanc.

# smoked foie gras with rhubarb and cinnamon purée and pommes allumettes

4 stalks rhubarb, cut into ¼-inch dice, but with trimmings reserved

1 stick cinnamon

⅓ cup sugar

2 Tbsp water

4 cups vegetable oil for deep frying

2 large Yukon Gold potatoes, 5 oz each, cut into matchsticks (allumettes) with a cross-section of ¼-inch square

4 slices foie gras, 3 oz each

2 tsp balsamic vinegar

*Serves 4*

To smoke the foie gras in this recipe you will need a sturdy pan with a lid and an insert like a small wire cooling rack. The pan heats the smoking sawdust while the insert supports the foie gras above the sawdust as it smoulders.

HEAT a medium sauté pan on medium heat. Add rhubarb trimmings, cinnamon stick, sugar and water and cook until rhubarb breaks down, about 10 minutes. Drain the liquid into a medium saucepan, bring to a boil and then reduce for 5 to 6 minutes on medium heat until large bubbles appear. Add diced rhubarb and allow to cool, then pour this mixture through a strainer to separate the syrup from the rhubarb dice. Purée the trimmings in a blender and pass through a fine sieve.

Heat oil in a deep-fryer or a deep pot to 250°F. Add potato allumettes and blanch for 3 minutes. Remove them from the oil and allow them to drain on paper towels.

Heat the pan you are using to smoke the foie gras on high heat until it is extremely hot. Add one handful of dry smoking sawdust into the pan, add the grill or insert, place the foie gras on the grill, cover and smoke for 5 minutes. Remove the lid and season the foie gras with salt and balsamic vinegar.

TO SERVE Place 2 tsp of purée at one end of each of four plates, then smear it across the plate with the back of a spoon. Heap a quarter of the allumettes at one end of the purée. Spoon a quarter of the syrup around the plate. Lay a slice of foie gras on top of the allumettes. Sprinkle a quarter of the rhubarb on top of and around the foie gras.

SUGGESTED WINE Sauternes is classic with foie gras, but with smoked foie gras a more powerful wine like a banyuls or Rivesaltes would be grand.

# wild spot prawns with citrus salad

2½ cups vegetable nage (page 228)

12 large spot prawns, washed and heads removed

1 small baguette (about 3 oz), frozen

2 Tbsp clarified butter (page 234)

1 pink grapefruit

1 orange

½ cup citrus dressing (page 236)

1 avocado, pitted, peeled and cut into ¾-inch dice

1 English cucumber, peeled, deseeded and cut into ¾-inch dice

2 oz mixed greens

*Serves 4*

In a medium saucepan, bring vegetable nage to a simmer and season with kosher salt. Place spot prawns into the simmering liquid and turn off heat. Let the prawns cool in the liquid.

Preheat the oven to 325°F.

Slice the baguette as thin as you can (about ⅛-inch thick) and brush with clarified butter. Freezing the baguette first will allow you to cut thin, even slices. Place in the oven and toast until golden brown, about 10 minutes.

Using a sharp knife, cut the peel off the grapefruit and orange and cut out the segments between the membranes. Dry the segments on a towel to remove excess liquid.

Peel spot prawns, place them in a bowl, season with salt and pepper and add 3 Tbsp of the citrus dressing.

In a small bowl, toss the avocado and cucumber with 3 Tbsp of the citrus dressing. In another bowl, toss the mixed greens with the remaining 2 Tbsp of citrus dressing.

TO SERVE  On each of four plates, lay out a quarter of the citrus segments, alternating between orange and grapefruit. Spoon a quarter of the cucumber and avocado around the citrus. Place three spot prawns and a quarter of the baguette slices onto the citrus and finish with mixed greens.

SUGGESTED WINE  The high acidity of the citrus can leave many wines feeling fat and flabby. Meet the acidity with B.C. bubbles, or harmonize the flavour with a New Zealand sauvignon blanc.

# ravioli of snails and truffles with sautéed spot prawns and shellfish jus

8 spot prawns

2 Tbsp unsalted butter

¼ onion, finely diced

1 clove garlic, finely chopped

1 tsp fresh thyme leaves

8 oz Bourgogne snails, halved

½ cup Madeira

1 cup roasting jus (page 232)

½ oz winter truffle, chopped

½ cup shellfish bisque (page 231)

8 oz pasta dough (page 237)

2 tsp olive oil

5 oz baby spinach leaves

2 Tbsp whipping cream

*Serves 4*

BRING a medium pot of salted water to a boil. Add prawns and blanch for 3 minutes until cooked. Plunge them into an ice bath to refresh, then peel and set aside.

In a small sauté pan, heat 4 tsp of the butter on medium heat. Add onion, garlic and thyme and cook until soft, about 2 minutes. Add snails and sauté for another 2 minutes. Add ¼ cup of the Madeira and cook until the liquid is reduced by two-thirds, about 4 minutes. Then add ½ cup of the roasting jus and again, cook 3 to 4 minutes until the liquid is reduced by two-thirds. Add truffle, then season with salt and pepper. Transfer this snail mixture to a bowl, allow to cool, then chill in the refrigerator until needed.

Add bisque and remaining ¼ cup of Madeira to the pan, then cook until reduced by two-thirds, about 5 minutes. Add the remaining ½ cup of the roasting jus and again, cook until reduced by two-thirds, about 5 minutes.

Roll pasta to the thickness of a dime or the lowest setting on a pasta machine in two 4-inch × 12-inch sheets. On one sheet of pasta, spoon twelve 2-tsp heaps of snail mixture along the centre line about every 1 inch. Moisten the pasta along the edges and between the fillings, then lay the other pasta sheet on top. Press down to seal between the fillings and along the edges, then cut between the fillings to yield twelve ravioli.

Bring a large pot of salted water to a boil. Add ravioli and cook for 5 minutes, then drain. In a small sauté pan, heat olive oil on medium heat and gently sauté spot prawns for 2 minutes on each side. Remove prawns from the pan, add the baby spinach and sauté for 10 to 12 seconds until just wilted.

Bring the Madeira shellfish jus to a boil, then add cream and whisk in the remaining 2 tsp of butter. Add ravioli and toss to coat.

TO SERVE In each of four bowls, heap a quarter of the spinach. Top with three ravioli and three prawns, then spoon Madeira shellfish jus overtop.

SUGGESTED WINE Macon or pouilly-fuissé would pair well with this dish's complex flavours.

# open ravioli of spot prawns and avocado
## with chilled tomato and basil consommé

TOMATO AND BASIL CONSOMMÉ

3 Tbsp olive oil

1½ carrots, chopped

1¼ small onions, chopped

3 ribs celery, chopped

½ small bulb fennel, chopped

1 leek, white part only, chopped

1 clove garlic, chopped

1 sprig thyme

1 bay leaf

8 ripe Roma tomatoes,
coarsely chopped

2 tsp tomato paste

4 cups water

1 chicken breast, about 4 oz

1 red beet, peeled
and coarsely chopped

2 egg whites

Stalks from 1–2 sprigs basil

*Serves 4*

TOMATO AND BASIL CONSOMMÉ   In a heavy bottomed sauté pan, heat olive oil on medium heat. Add 1 carrot, 1 onion, 2 ribs celery, fennel, leek, garlic, thyme and bay leaf and roast until soft, about 10 minutes. Add tomatoes, cover the pan and cook for a further 10 minutes. Add tomato paste and cook for 1 minute. Cover the mixture with water and bring to a boil, then reduce heat to low and simmer for 45 minutes.

Strain this tomato stock through a cheesecloth and chill in the refrigerator until cold.

In a food processor, blend together chicken breast, the remaining ½ carrot, ¼ onion, 1 rib celery and the beet and egg whites to make a clarification. Transfer this mixture to a medium saucepan and whisk in cold tomato stock. Place the saucepan on medium heat, stirring continuously until the clarification rises and sets on top of the stock. Break a small hole in the surface of the clarification and simmer gently for 20 minutes. Strain the stock through a cheesecloth and add basil stalks to infuse. Chill in the refrigerator for at least 1 hour.

SPOT PRAWN AND AVOCADO FILLING   Bring a small pot of salted water to a boil. Add prawns and blanch for 15 seconds. Remove the prawns from the water and peel them.

In a medium non-reactive bowl, combine orange juice, lime juice, lime zest, chili, cilantro and olive oil. Add prawns and marinate for at least 1 hour.

In a small bowl, crush avocado with a fork. Season with lemon juice, Tabasco and a pinch of salt and pepper.

*Recipe continued overleaf. . .*

12 spot prawns, heads removed

Juice of 1 orange

Juice of 1 lime

Zest of 1 lime

½ red chili, very finely chopped

10 cilantro leaves, chopped

1½ Tbsp olive oil

1 ripe avocado, pitted and peeled

Juice of 1 lemon

Dash of Tabasco

RAVIOLI PASTA

8 basil leaves

8 oz pasta dough (page 237)

RAVIOLI PASTA  Bring a small pot of salted water to a boil. Add basil leaves and blanch for 5 seconds, then remove them from the pot and plunge them into an ice bath to refresh. Allow them to dry on a paper towel.

Roll out pasta dough to a ¹⁄₁₆-inch thickness. Lay out the basil leaves over one half of the pasta sheet, then fold the other half overtop to sandwich the leaves in the pasta. Roll this pasta sheet to the thickness of a dime.

Line a baking sheet with plastic wrap. Cut the pasta sheet into eight 2½-inch squares. Bring a small pot of salted water to a boil. Add pasta squares and blanch for 2 minutes, then immediately plunge them into an ice bath to refresh. Lay the squares out on the lined baking sheet and brush each square gently with oil. Cover with plastic wrap and store in the refrigerator until ready to serve.

TO SERVE  In each of four bowls, place one square of pasta, then top with 1 tsp of avocado filling. Cut each prawn in half and lay six prawn halves on top of the avocado. Cover with a second square of pasta. Ladle a quarter of the consommé around the ravioli and serve.

SUGGESTED WINE  Think pink. The delicate flavour of the marinated sweet prawns are well complemented by a young, crisp, dry B.C. rosé. Its raspberry and strawberry notes contrast nicely with the tomato and basil consommé. The heavier, more pungent Tavel rosés would also work well.

**IN LATE SPRING** Vancouver welcomes the B.C. Spot Prawn Festival, where chefs and home cooks alike take advantage of the opportunity to buy spot prawns fresh off docked fishing boats. Yes, the prawns have spots, small and white, usually on the second and fifth sections of their abdominal area. They are protandic hermaphroditic creatures: they begin life as males, and each individual undergoes a transition into a female near the end of its four-year life expectancy. They are caught in line-held traps that sit on the ocean's bottom, normally two to three hundred feet below the surface.

The seasonal window is six to eight precious weeks, and 90 per cent of the commercial catch goes directly to Japan. So the arrival of spot prawns is clearly a time for celebration, since their firm, delicate meat has come to exemplify what the words "local" and "seasonal" actually mean in a culinary context.

# spot prawns

pan-fried halibut and chanterelles
with watercress sauce and lasagna of crab

# pan-fried halibut and chanterelles with watercress sauce and lasagna of crab

16 cups court bouillon (page 229)

1 small Dungeness crab, about 2 lbs

4 oz pasta dough (page 237)

2 oz chicken mousse (page 233)

WATERCRESS SAUCE

7 oz watercress, leaves
picked off and stems discarded

⅓ cup chicken stock (page 231)

1 tsp olive oil

1 shallot, chopped

PAN-FRIED HALIBUT

2 tsp olive oil

4 fillets halibut, about 4 oz each

½ lemon

2 tsp unsalted butter

3 oz yellowfoot chanterelle
mushrooms

DEEP-FRIED WATERCRESS

1 cup vegetable oil for deep frying

4 sprigs watercress, leaves
picked off and stems discarded

*Serves 4*

CRAB LASAGNA  In a large pot, bring court bouillon to a boil. Add crab and cook for 12 minutes. Remove from heat and allow the crab to cool in the bouillon. Pick the crab meat from the shell: first, twist off the legs and claws and set them aside. To remove the back, hold the base of the crab with one hand and pull the shell away from the body with the other hand. Discard the soft gills and the intestine. Spoon out the soft brown meat and reserve. Gently rinse the crab shell and crack it into four pieces. Pick out all of the crab's white meat—from the legs, claws and rest of the body. Break crab shells into 1½- to 2-inch pieces.

Roll out pasta dough to the thickness of a dime. Bring a large pot of salted water to a boil. Add pasta, blanch for 3 minutes, then refresh in an ice bath. Cut out twelve 1½-inch-diameter rounds.

In a small bowl, mix white crab meat with brown meat and chicken mousse. Season with salt and pepper.

Grease four 1½-inch ring moulds. In each one, lay down a pasta round, top with one-eighth of the crab, another pasta round, another eighth of the crab and a third pasta round.

WATERCRESS SAUCE  Bring a medium saucepan of water to a boil. Add watercress and blanch for 15 seconds. Plunge the watercress into an ice bath to refresh, then squeeze out the excess water and chop.

Bring chicken stock to a boil in a small saucepan.

In a small sauté pan, heat oil on medium heat. Add shallot and sweat 2 to 3 minutes but do not brown. Add watercress and just cover with boiling chicken stock. Cook until the watercress and shallot are tender, 2 to 3 minutes, then purée in a blender, pass through a sieve, and season with salt and pepper.

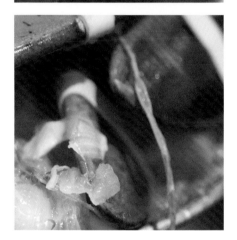

PAN-FRIED HALIBUT  In a large, non-stick pan on high heat, add olive oil, then add halibut and fry for 3 to 4 minutes on each side. Season with salt and pepper and a squeeze of lemon juice.

Melt some butter in a small sauté pan on low heat, add mushrooms and gently cook for 2 to 3 minutes. Season with salt and pepper.

DEEP-FRIED WATERCRESS  Heat oil in a deep fryer or a small saucepan to 400°F. Immerse watercress leaves and fry for 3 to 4 seconds. Remove the watercress from the oil and allow to drain on paper towels.

TO SERVE  Place crab lasagna in a steamer and cook for 7 to 8 minutes.

Into each of four pasta bowls, spoon a quarter of the watercress sauce. Place a lasagna in a centre of the bowl and top with a fillet of halibut. Sprinkle a quarter of the yellowfoot chanterelles around the lasagna and garnish the dish with the deep-fried watercress.

SUGGESTED WINE  Try an intense but balanced chardonnay from southern B.C., Washington State or California (Carneros or Russian River). The caramelized flavours the fish gets from pan frying and the buttery texture of the chanterelles work well with some (but not too much) oak flavour and a rich texture in the wine.

# roasted fillet of ling cod with spicy braised pork belly and caramelized butternut squash

1 carrot, roughly chopped

1 onion, roughly chopped

2 cloves garlic, roughly chopped

2 ribs celery, roughly chopped

1 sprig thyme, leaves
picked off and stem discarded

2 bay leaves

2 tsp Chinese five-spice powder

⅓ cup white wine

4 cups chicken stock (page 231)

1 lb pork belly, skinned
and halved lengthwise

3 tsp olive oil

1 tsp unsalted butter

TARRAGON POLENTA

4 cups chicken stock (page 231)

⅓ cup stone-ground white polenta

2 oz Parmigiano-Reggiano,
grated (about ½ cup)

3 Tbsp unsalted butter

½ oz tarragon, chopped
(about 2 Tbsp)

*Serves 4*

SPICY BRAISED PORK  Preheat the oven to 275°F. Combine carrot, onion, garlic, celery, thyme, bay leaves and five-spice powder in a heavy-bottomed roasting pan. Place in the oven and roast for 15 minutes. Remove from the oven and add wine and chicken stock to complete the braising liquid. Heat on the stove until liquid reaches a boil, then remove from heat.

Roll and tie pork belly into two cylinders, 2 inches in diameter, and place in the roasting pan with the braising liquid. Place in the oven and cook for 1½ to 2 hours until the pork is tender. Remove the pork from the pan, remove and discard the string and wrap the pork tightly in parchment paper, then foil, and allow to set in the refrigerator overnight. Strain the braising liquid through a sieve into a small saucepan. Heat on medium heat until reduced to the consistency of cream, about 45 minutes. Adjust seasoning with salt and pepper.

TARRAGON POLENTA  Bring chicken stock to a boil. Add polenta and stir. Allow to cook on low heat, stirring occasionally, until all of the grains are soft, 2 to 3 hours.

CARAMELIZED BUTTERNUT SQUASH  Cut the neck of the butternut squash into twelve ½-inch slices, then cut each slice into a disc 1 to 1½ inches in diameter.

Heat a large non-stick pan on high heat. Add olive oil and butter, then add butternut squash discs and cook until golden brown on each side, about 3 minutes per side.

CARAMELIZED BUTTERNUT SQUASH

1 butternut squash with
a long neck, about 1 lb

2 tsp olive oil

2 tsp unsalted butter

ROASTED LING COD

2 tsp olive oil

4 fillets ling cod, 5½ oz each

FRIED TARRAGON GARNISH

1 cup vegetable oil for deep frying

2 sprigs tarragon, leaves
picked off and stems discarded

ROASTED LING COD  Preheat the oven to 350°F.

Heat a medium ovenproof sauté pan on high heat. Add olive oil, then add ling cod fillets, skin-side down. Place in the oven and cook for 3 to 4 minutes. Season with salt and pepper.

FRIED TARRAGON GARNISH  Heat oil in a deep fryer or a medium saucepan to 400°F. Immerse tarragon leaves in the oil for 3 to 4 seconds, then remove from the oil and drain on paper towels.

TO SERVE  Cut the pork belly into slices about ½ inch thick. Heat a large non-stick pan on high heat. Add olive oil and butter, then add pork slices and cook gently until lightly brown on each side, about 2 minutes per side.

Stir Parmigiano-Reggiano, butter and tarragon into polenta. Season to taste with salt and pepper.

Down the centre of each of four plates, spoon a quarter of the polenta into a strip about 1 inch wide and 4 inches long. Alternately arrange three pork slices and three butternut squash discs on the polenta. Top with a fillet of ling cod. Spoon the sauce around and garnish with fried tarragon.

SUGGESTED WINE  You will need a rich white with neutral oak and a bit of residual sugar to pair with this meaty fish and the spice of the pork. Try a kabinett or spätlese German riesling from the Mosel or the Rheingau. Red wine lovers should try a light red with soft, gentle tannins, like Oregon pinot noir or Bourgeuil from the Loire.

# herb-crusted saddle of new season lamb with sweet and sour shallots

HERB-CRUSTED LAMB

3 oz fresh bread crumbs

1 sprig thyme, leaves
picked off and chopped

1 oz parsley, chopped (about ¼ cup)

1½ oz Gruyère cheese, grated

¼ cup unsalted butter,
softened at room temperature

1 saddle of lamb, about 4 lbs

½ onion, sliced

3 cloves garlic, crushed

1 rib celery, sliced

1 carrot, sliced

5 tsp white wine vinegar

2 Roma tomatoes, cut into eighths

1 tsp tomato paste

1 sprig rosemary

8 cups chicken stock (page 231)

1 egg white

⅔ cup whipping cream

*Serves 6*

This recipe calls for duck fat, which adds a very refined, rich flavour to most dishes. At West, we render duck fat from our organic ducks and use it where you would clarified butter. It's easy to make but is also available from most butchers or specialty food stores.

HERB-CRUSTED LAMB  Make a herb crust by combining bread crumbs, thyme and parsley in a food processor. Let the machine work for 2 minutes until the bread crumbs turn bright green. Add Gruyère, then slowly add butter and season with salt. Place this mixture between two pieces of parchment paper and roll out to ¼ inch in thickness. Place in the freezer for at least 1 hour.

Remove as much fat as possible from the saddle of lamb without breaking through and exposing meat. Remove the tenderloins and set them aside, then remove the backbone very carefully, using a sharp boning knife. You should be left with one piece of boneless saddle and two loins. Refrigerate the loins.

Preheat the oven to 375°F. Cut all of the bones, trim them into 2½-inch pieces and place them in a roasting pan. Roast in the oven until golden brown, about 45 minutes. Add onion, garlic, celery and carrot and roast for another 20 minutes, then deglaze the pan with white wine vinegar. Add tomatoes, tomato paste and rosemary and roast a further 10 minutes, then drain off excess fat. Place roasted bones in a large pot and cover with chicken stock, topping off with water until the bones are just covered. Simmer for 2 hours, strain the liquid through a fine sieve into a medium saucepan, and continue heating until reduced by four-fifths, about 1 hour.

In a food processor, purée tenderloins with egg white and slowly add cream. Pass this mixture through a fine sieve, season with salt and pepper and set this tenderloin mousse aside.

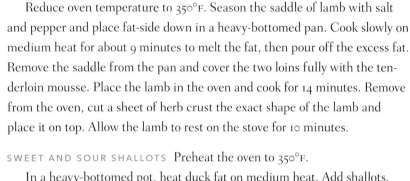

1 Tbsp duck fat

18 large shallots

1 sprig thyme

1 bay leaf

3½ Tbsp sherry vinegar

⅓ cup chicken stock (page 231)

Reduce oven temperature to 350°F. Season the saddle of lamb with salt and pepper and place fat-side down in a heavy-bottomed pan. Cook slowly on medium heat for about 9 minutes to melt the fat, then pour off the excess fat. Remove the saddle from the pan and cover the two loins fully with the tenderloin mousse. Place the lamb in the oven and cook for 14 minutes. Remove from the oven, cut a sheet of herb crust the exact shape of the lamb and place it on top. Allow the lamb to rest on the stove for 10 minutes.

SWEET AND SOUR SHALLOTS  Preheat the oven to 350°F.

In a heavy-bottomed pot, heat duck fat on medium heat. Add shallots, thyme, bay leaf and salt and roast until shallots are golden brown all over, about 15 minutes. Deglaze with sherry vinegar and chicken stock and bring to a simmer. Place in the oven for 15 minutes or until the shallots are soft to the touch. Strain the liquid into a small saucepan and simmer on medium heat until reduced to a glaze, about 3 minutes. Add the shallots to the glaze and keep warm.

TO SERVE  Return the lamb to the 350°F oven for 4 minutes. Warm six plates. With a very sharp, clean knife, slice lamb into six equal pieces. On each of the plates, place a piece of lamb in the middle, then spoon the shallots and sauce around.

SUGGESTED WINE  A well-structured medium- to full-bodied red with intense fruit will link well with the savoury and sweet flavours of the dish. Rioja and Ribera del Duero are classic pairings, but this dish also offers an opportunity to try more rustic wines from southwest France like Madiran, Cahors or Bergerac, which are country cousins of Bordeaux.

# saddle of lamb with caramelized onion purée, croquettes and sticky lamb with crisp tongues

LAMB SHOULDER AND TONGUES

2 pieces lamb shoulder
on bone, ½ lb each

4 tsp vegetable oil

2 Tbsp unsalted butter

2 carrots, chopped

1 onion, chopped

4 ribs celery, chopped

2 cloves garlic, chopped

2 sprigs thyme

¾ cup red wine

2 cups chicken stock (page 231)

2 lamb tongues, soaked
in cold water for 24 hours

2 tsp balsamic vinegar

¾ cup flour

4 cups vegetable oil for deep frying

LAMB SADDLE

1 lamb saddle, about 2½ lbs,
split lengthwise down the bone

*Serves 4*

LAMB SHOULDER AND TONGUES   Preheat the oven to 275°F. Season the lamb shoulder well with salt and pepper. Heat vegetable oil and butter in a heavy-bottomed, ovenproof pan on high heat. Add lamb shoulder and sear until browned, about 12 minutes. Remove the shoulder and set aside.

Add carrots, onion, celery, garlic and thyme to the hot pan and roast until browned, about 6 minutes. Add wine, then cook until it is reduced by half, about 10 minutes. Add chicken stock and bring to a boil. Add shoulder and tongues and cover the pan. Place the pan in the oven and cook for 2 to 3 hours until tender. Remove the tongues, peel and set aside in the refrigerator. Remove the meat from bone of the shoulder and place in a medium sauté pan. Strain the braising liquid through a sieve, pouring half into a small saucepan and the other half into the pan with the shoulder meat. Heat the meat on medium heat for 20 to 25 minutes until the glaze is sticky. Season with salt, pepper and balsamic vinegar.

Cook the braising liquid in the saucepan on medium heat until reduced to the consistency of cream, about 25 minutes.

Thinly slice the lamb tongues lengthwise and dredge the slices in flour.

LAMB SADDLE   Preheat the oven to 350°F. Season lamb saddle well with salt and pepper. Heat a heavy-bottomed ovenproof pan on high heat. Add lamb saddle and sear until caramelized all over, about 2 minutes per side, then place in the oven for 10 to 12 minutes. Remove from heat and allow to rest for 10 to 12 minutes.

Remove the lamb from the bone. Cut the fillet into four pieces and slice each loin into ten pieces.

2 egg yolks

2 Yukon Gold potatoes,
5 oz each, baked and passed
through a ricer while still warm

Pinch of ground nutmeg

1 egg

1¼ cups bread crumbs

ONION PURÉE

2 tsp olive oil

1½ Tbsp unsalted butter

1 onion, chopped

5 Tbsp brown veal and
chicken jus (page 232)

BRAISED LEEKS

2 leeks, white parts only,
cut into ½-inch segments

¾ cup chicken stock (page 231)

4 tsp unsalted butter

CROQUETTES  Fold one of the egg yolks into the potato. Season with nutmeg, salt and pepper. Roll this potato mixture into 1-inch-diameter balls.

Lightly beat together egg, remaining egg yolk and a pinch of salt. Dip the potato balls first in egg wash, then in the bread crumbs. Store these balls in an airtight container until ready to fry.

ONION PURÉE  In a heavy-bottomed pan, heat olive oil and butter on medium heat until butter turns brown and smells nutty, about 2 minutes. Add onion and cook until soft and brown, about 12 minutes. Add brown veal and chicken jus. Purée in a blender and pass through a sieve, then season with salt and pepper.

BRAISED LEEKS  In a medium pot, combine leeks, chicken stock, butter and salt and pepper. Cover the leeks with a cartouche—a round of parchment paper cut to the diameter of the pot, with a hole in the centre to allow steam to escape—and braise the leeks on medium heat for 8 to 10 minutes.

TO SERVE  Heat vegetable oil in a deep fryer or a deep pot to 350°F. Place the potato balls and the tongue slices into the hot oil and cook until crisp and brown, about 2 minutes, then drain on paper towels.

Spoon 1 tsp of the purée into an arc along the edge of each of four plates and arrange croquettes evenly along this arc. Heap a quarter of the leeks into the centre of the plate and a quarter of the braised lamb to the side. Fan out a quarter of the sliced lamb along the edge of the braised lamb. Top with a quarter of the tongue slices then spoon a quarter of the sauce overtop and around the plate.

SUGGESTED WINE  Washington syrah has been getting better and better with each vintage, and with its voluptuous mouth feel and round, supple tannin, it is perfect with this lamb dish.

ABOVE: saddle of lamb with caramelized onion
purée, croquettes and sticky lamb with crisp tongues
RIGHT: veal and tuna with olive panisse

# veal and tuna with olive panisse

### OLIVE PANISSE

5 oz chickpea flour (about 1 cup)

⅓ cup extra-virgin olive oil

3 Tbsp tapenade (page 150)

2 cups water

1 tsp kosher salt

### TUNA SAUCE

½ cup peanut oil

½ cup extra-virgin olive oil

4 oz albacore tuna trim

2 egg yolks

1 hard-boiled egg yolk

1 Tbsp Dijon mustard

4 anchovy fillets

1 clove garlic

1 Tbsp capers

*Serves 4*

This dish is a twist on the classic vitello tonnato. For it you will need shiso leaves—available at Asian supermarkets—and chickpea flour—available in specialty food stores. The olive panisse can be made up to 3 days in advance.

OLIVE PANISSE In a medium mixing bowl, combine 1 cup of the chickpea flour with the olive oil, tapenade, water and salt to form a thick batter. (A spoon drawn through the batter should leave a trail that slowly falls back together. If the batter is too thin, gradually add more chickpea flour until it reaches the right consistency). Cook for about 15 minutes on medium heat in a heavy-bottomed pot, stirring constantly. Place the chickpea mixture between two sheets of parchment, roll to about ¾ inches in thickness, wrap in plastic wrap and chill in the refrigerator for at least 3 hours.

Cut into ¾-inch cubes.

TUNA SAUCE Combine peanut and olive oils in a medium pot and warm to 175°F—confirm the temperature with a thermometer. Add tuna trim and cook about 3 minutes or until fully cooked. Remove the cooked tuna with a slotted spoon and allow the oil to cool to room temperature.

In a food processor, purée raw and cooked egg yolks, mustard, anchovy fillets, garlic, cooked tuna trim and the capers until fully emulsified.

In a slow, steady stream, pour in the oil while continuing to process the mixture. Season with salt and pepper and chill in the refrigerator for 1 hour or up to 3 days in advance.

VEAL AND TUNA Bring a medium pot of water to a boil. Add asparagus and blanch for 20 seconds. Remove from the boiling water and plunge into an ice bath. Next, blanch green onions for 40 seconds. Plunge those into an ice bath to halt the cooking and retain the colour.

8 asparagus spears

4 green onions

4 veal fillets, 4 oz each

8 shiso leaves

4 pieces albacore tuna, 2½ oz each

2 Tbsp extra-virgin olive oil

4 cups vegetable oil for frying

3 Tbsp capers

micro basil for garnish

Place each veal fillet between two sheets of plastic wrap and gently flatten with a kitchen mallet to a ¼-inch thickness.

On a piece of plastic wrap 8 inches × 8 inches, lay down one veal fillet, followed by two shiso leaves on top. Next, lay down two spears of asparagus (pointing in opposite directions), one green onion and one piece of tuna. Roll the veal fillet tightly around this filling and wrap the veal in the plastic wrap, tying off the ends to seal. Repeat for all veal fillets. Allow to set in the refrigerator overnight or for 8 to 12 hours.

Preheat the oven to 375°F.

Remove the plastic wrap from the veal and season the veal with salt and pepper. Heat olive oil in a large, ovenproof sauté pan on medium heat. Add veal and sear until golden brown on all sides, about 4 minutes. Place in the oven for 2 minutes. Remove from heat and allow to rest.

TO SERVE Heat vegetable oil to 350°F. Add capers and fry until crispy, about 20 seconds. Remove from the oil and drain on a paper towel. Add panisse to the hot oil and fry until golden brown and crisp, about 60 seconds. Remove from the oil and season with salt and pepper.

Cut veal into slices 1¼ inches thick. In the middle of each of four plates, spoon a quarter of the tuna sauce. Place a quarter of the veal and a quarter of the panisse on the sauce and garnish with the micro basil and fried capers.

SUGGESTED WINE Although many white wines are great with both tuna and veal, this tasty dish is best with red. The savoury, spicy characteristics of a reserva Rioja or a barbaresco would complement the complex flavours of the dish and also have the structure to balance the salty ingredients. A good dark Belgian beer is also an excellent match.

# meyer lemon crêpe roll with chiffon and coconut buckwheat honey ice cream

## LEMON MARMALADE

2 Meyer lemons

1 cup sugar

1 cup water

## CRÊPES

4 tsp unsalted butter

½ cup whole milk

1 Tbsp sugar

1 egg

1 egg yolk

1 Tbsp vanilla extract

1 Tbsp vegetable oil

¾ cup flour

## COCONUT-LEMON CHIFFON

4 eggs, separated

½ cup sugar

3 Tbsp + 1 tsp lemon juice

1 tsp lemon reduction (page 236)

1 Tbsp Cointreau

4 gelatin leaves, softened in a little cold water

¾ cup grated coconut, toasted and allowed to cool

*Serves 9*

Meyer lemons are not as sour as regular lemons and they have a distinct flavour. They are available, usually in late winter or early spring, at specialty produce stores. Coconut purée can also be purchased at specialty stores, but if you cannot find it, coconut milk will make a fine substitute. Buckwheat honey, available anywhere with a wide selection of different honeys, lends this dessert a very earthy flavour—feel free to substitute other honeys, but be aware that the taste will not be the same.

This dessert, as well as many others at West, features tuiles, which are wafer-thin cookies that can be made into different shapes using templates. Tuile templates, which are essentially stencils for the cookie batter, are available at kitchen supply stores, but you can easily make a template by cutting the desired shape out of a piece of thin, flat plastic, like the lid of a yogurt container. The thin batter is spread into the voids of the template with a small offset spatula, and the template is removed, leaving a cookie of the desired shape.

LEMON MARMALADE  Cut lemons into ¼-inch slices and remove seeds. Place lemons, sugar and water into a small saucepan and simmer 30 to 40 minutes until mixture becomes thick and syrupy. Allow to cool, then chop very fine.

CRÊPES  In a small saucepan, heat butter on medium heat until it is light brown and gives off a nutty aroma, about 4 minutes.

In a blender, mix milk, sugar, egg, egg yolk, vanilla, oil and flour until well blended. Add hot brown butter and blend for 5 more seconds.

Heat a small non-stick sauté pan on medium heat. Pour about 2 Tbsp of batter onto the pan, tilting it to make sure that the mixture covers the bottom and reaches the sides of the pan. Cook until batter has set, about 30 seconds, then flip the crêpe over and cook for about 10 more seconds. Remove

COCONUT TUILES

¼ cup unsalted butter, melted

¾ cup icing sugar

½ cup coconut milk

1 cup flour

⅓ cup egg whites
(about 2½ large eggs)

ICE CREAM

2 Tbsp buckwheat honey

½ cup whole milk

1 cup whipping cream

1 cup coconut purée

4 egg yolks

⅓ cup sugar

the crêpe from the pan and slide onto a plate. Repeat until all of the batter is cooked; use a piece of parchment paper to separate each crêpe in the stack of finished crêpes.

COCONUT–LEMON CHIFFON Lightly grease an 8-inch square dish and line it with parchment paper. In a stainless-steel bowl, combine egg yolks, ¼ cup of the sugar, lemon juice, lemon reduction and Cointreau and whisk over a pot of gently simmering water until the mixture is thick, fluffy and hot to the touch, about 3 minutes. Wring the gelatin to remove excess moisture and gently fold it into the mixture.

In another bowl, whisk egg whites with the remaining ¼ cup of sugar until stiff peaks form. Fold into the lemon mixture. Pour batter onto the parchment-lined dish. Refrigerate for 2 hours or until set.

Slice into 2½-inch squares and toss in grated coconut to coat. Store in an airtight container in the refrigerator until needed.

COCONUT TUILES Preheat oven to 350°F. In a stainless-steel bowl, combine butter and sugar and whisk until smooth. Whisk in coconut milk, flour and egg whites.

Line a baking sheet with a silicone mat or parchment paper.

Using an offset spatula, spread the coconut tuile batter across a 2½-inch square template. Lift the template, leaving a square of batter. Repeat until you have made eighteen tuiles.

Bake for 5 minutes or until golden brown.

Allow to cool to room temperature. Tuiles may be made in advance and stored in an airtight container for up to 2 weeks.

*Recipe continued overleaf. . .*

ICE CREAM Chill an 8-inch square pan in the freezer. In a medium saucepan, bring honey, milk, cream and coconut purée to a boil, stirring occasionally to make sure that the mixture doesn't burn on the bottom.

In a medium stainless-steel bowl, whisk egg yolks and sugar until the mixture becomes a pale yellow. Add hot cream mixture to egg yolks while whisking constantly.

Return this custard to the saucepan and cook on high heat, stirring constantly, until the custard coats the back of a spoon, about 15 minutes. Cool the saucepan over ice. Pour custard into an ice cream machine and process according to the manufacturer's instructions. Spread onto the chilled pan and freeze for 12 hours. Cut into 2½-inch squares.

TO SERVE Spread a thin layer of marmalade onto each crêpe and roll it into a cigar shape. Cut off the two tips so that the ends are flat. Set aside.

On each of nine plates, place a tuile. Place a square of ice cream on the tuile, then top with another tuile to make an ice cream sandwich. Place a square of chiffon on top.

Lay the crêpe roll on top, diagonally across the square.

SUGGESTED WINE The lemon marmalade is both sweet and acidic, so a wine that has complementary acidity but a higher sweetness—as found in a high-quality Sauternes—will pair very well. The toasty vanilla oak flavours of Sauternes would also play nicely with the coconut flavours in the chiffon and the ice cream.

MERINGUE  Combine egg whites, sugar and lemon zest in a medium stainless-steel bowl. Place the bowl over a pot of simmering water and whisk the mixture until it is fluffy and hot to the touch, about 3 minutes. Remove from heat and whisk until cool. Transfer meringue to a piping bag with a star tip. The meringue can be made up to 24 hours in advance and stored, in the piping bag, in the refrigerator.

TO SERVE  In the middle of each of six plates, spoon one tablespoon of the caramel sauce. Top with a tuile, followed by another tablespoon of caramel sauce and another tuile.

Unmould each frozen soufflé by running a hot knife along the edge of the mould. Place a soufflé on top of the tuiles. Pipe a sixth of the meringue on top of the frozen soufflé and quickly heat the meringue with a kitchen torch to caramelize the surface.

SUGGESTED WINE  Try a Canadian riesling icewine. Icewine is a dessert in itself—so sweet and intense that pairing it with dessert is usually redundant. But in this case, its sweet golden apple/stone-fruit character and acidity complement the tamarind and lemon flavours nicely, while the dessert's freezing temperature can't resist the icewine's warming sweetness. A vidal icewine would make a very nice match as well.

RHUBARB can conjure up memories of fecund plants growing with wild abandon, taking over entire sections of a backyard garden and resulting in a harvest that meant a dreaded onslaught of either too-bitter or over-sweetened stews, pies, cakes, muffins and breads. It is not a fruit but a vegetable, though some sources even identify it as an herb, with cousins like sorrel and buckwheat in its family.

Emperor Wu in the Liang Dynasty used it as a cure for fever, so rhubarb's roots are noble and ancient. Marco Polo brought it to Europe, and the underappreciated vegetable made its way to North America in the late eighteenth century. Spring harvest is best, before the leaves begin to yellow and the stalks begin to lose their firmness. The leaves are poisonous, but the dark red stalks have a marvellous flavour and tangy, almost citrusy effect and can be used in a wide array of dishes, not only in those ubiquitous pies and tarts. You might even find them in a cocktail somewhere.

rhubarb

# poached rhubarb with rhubarb sorbet, basmati rice cream and citrus semolina cake

## RHUBARB SORBET

7 oz rhubarb, thinly sliced

¾ cup sugar syrup (page 235)

¼ cup corn syrup

## POACHED RHUBARB

10 oz rhubarb, sliced

⅓ cup white wine

½ vanilla bean, split and scraped, but pod reserved

1 cup sugar

## BASMATI RICE CREAM

¼ cup basmati rice

1¼ cups whole milk

¼ vanilla bean, split and scraped, but pod reserved

⅓ cup sugar

¾ cup whipping cream

*Serves 6*

RHUBARB SORBET  Purée rhubarb, sugar syrup and corn syrup in a blender. Strain mixture through a sieve then pour into an ice cream machine and process according to the manufacturer's instructions. Store 8 to 12 hours or overnight in the coldest part of the freezer.

POACHED RHUBARB  Preheat the oven to 350°F. Place rhubarb, wine, vanilla bean (both seeds and pod) and sugar in a roasting pan. Cover with foil and cook in the oven for 30 minutes, or until rhubarb is tender. Remove and discard the vanilla pod. Allow rhubarb to cool and store in the refrigerator.

BASMATI RICE CREAM  In a medium saucepan, bring rice, milk and vanilla bean (both seeds and pod) to a simmer. Cook until rice is soft and over-cooked, about 30 minutes. Add sugar. Remove and discard the vanilla pod. Purée rice mixture in a blender, strain through a sieve and allow to cool.

In a large bowl, whip cream to stiff peaks, then fold into the rice mixture.

CITRUS SEMOLINA CAKE  In a small saucepan, make a syrup by combining the lemon juice, orange juice and vanilla. Add ¼ cup of the sugar and the water. Bring to a boil, cook for 1 minute, then remove from heat and allow to cool.

Line a baking sheet with parchment paper and preheat the oven to 350°F.

In a bowl, sift together all-purpose flour, baking powder and semolina flour.

## CITRUS SEMOLINA CAKE

Juice and zest of 1 lemon

Juice and zest of 1 orange

1 tsp vanilla extract

¾ cup sugar

¼ cup water

⅓ cup all-purpose flour

1 tsp baking powder

⅓ cup semolina flour

⅔ cup unsalted butter

3 eggs, separated

⅓ cup sweet wine,
like Essensia orange muscat

In the bowl of an electric mixer, cream together butter, lemon zest, orange zest and the remaining ½ cup of sugar until fluffy and light in colour. Add egg yolks one at a time. Add a third of the flour mixture, followed by a third of the sweet wine. Repeat until all of the flour and wine has been incorporated.

In another mixing bowl, whisk egg whites to stiff peaks. Fold them into the batter.

Pour cake batter onto the baking sheet. Bake until light golden on the edges and soft to the touch, about 20 minutes. Pour citrus syrup over the cake and allow to cool. Using a round cutter 2½ inches in diameter, cut out six rounds of cake.

TO SERVE   Onto each of six plates, scoop a heaping spoonful of basmati rice cream, then place a citrus cake on top. Pile a sixth of the poached rhubarb next to the cake and top with a ¼-cup scoop of sorbet. Drizzle some of the rhubarb poaching liquid onto the cake and the rhubarb.

SUGGESTED WINE   A sweet Champagne is a playful choice for this dessert. The Champagne's natural cool-climate tang handles the rhubarb with aplomb—and the pear and citrus flavours of the wine also complement the citrus semolina cake well. For a still wine match, try a late-harvest riesling from B.C. or Ontario, or a vendange tardive riesling from Alsace.

# rhubarb tatin with ginger ice cream, poached apple and brown sugar sauce

### PÂTE BRISÉE

4¼ cups flour

1 tsp salt

1 lb + 2 oz cold unsalted butter, cut into ¾-inch cubes

1⅓ cups cold water

### PASTRY CREAM

3 egg yolks

½ tsp vanilla extract

⅓ cup sugar

4 tsp flour

1 cup whole milk

### GINGER ICE CREAM

1 cup whole milk

1 cup whipping cream

4 egg yolks

½ cup sugar

½ tsp vanilla extract

½ oz candied ginger, finely diced (about 2 tsp)

*Serves 6*

This dish includes a recipe for pâte brisée, one of the most versatile types of pastry dough; leftover pâte brisée will freeze very well.

PÂTE BRISÉE  In a large mixing bowl, combine flour, salt and butter with a pastry blender until the mixture resembles a coarse meal. Add water and mix until dough comes together.

Chill in the refrigerator for 1 hour.

Line a baking sheet with parchment paper. On a floured surface, roll out the dough to a ¼-inch thickness. Cut rounds 3 inches in diameter, place them on the baking sheet and chill for about 1 hour.

Preheat the oven to 375°F.

Top the rounds of dough with another layer of parchment paper, followed by another baking sheet, and bake until pale golden, about 20 minutes. Remove from the oven and allow to cool.

PASTRY CREAM  In a medium heatproof mixing bowl, whisk together egg yolks, vanilla and sugar until the mixture is a pale yellow. Whisk in the flour.

In a medium saucepan, bring milk to a boil. Slowly add hot milk to egg yolks, whisking constantly. Return the custard to the pan and whisk for 10 more seconds. Remove from heat, cover the custard's surface with plastic wrap to prevent a skin from forming, then cool the saucepan over an ice bath.

Pour the custard into a bowl, cover with plastic wrap to prevent a skin from forming on the surface and refrigerate.

GINGER ICE CREAM  In a medium saucepan, bring milk and cream to a boil. Meanwhile, whisk together egg yolks, sugar and vanilla in a medium heatproof bowl until the mixture becomes a pale yellow. Slowly add hot milk mixture to egg yolks, whisking constantly. Return this custard to the saucepan and cook on high heat, stirring, until the mixture coats the back of a

1 Pink Lady apple

1 cup apple juice

⅓ cup sugar

Juice of 1 lemon

¼ vanilla bean, split and
scraped, but pod reserved

1 lb + 2 oz rhubarb, cut
into strips 1/4 inch wide

BROWN SUGAR SAUCE

½ cup brown sugar

⅓ cup half & half cream

½ tsp vanilla extract

1 Tbsp unsalted butter, melted

spoon. Remove the saucepan from heat and cool over ice. Pour the custard into an electric ice cream maker and process according to the manufacturer's instructions. Fold in candied ginger. Freeze until needed.

POACHED APPLE AND RHUBARB TART TOPPINGS  Cut slices ½ inch thick from the sides of the apple. Cut out 2-inch rounds.

In a small saucepan, combine apple juice, sugar, lemon juice and vanilla bean (both seeds and pod). Add apple rounds and bring to a simmer. Cook until a knife easily pierces the apple pieces, about 20 minutes.

Remove apples with a slotted spoon and set aside. Continue to cook the liquid until reduced by half, about 10 minutes. Return apples to the liquid and allow to cool. Remove and discard the vanilla pod.

BROWN SUGAR SAUCE  Whisk together brown sugar, cream and vanilla in a stainless-steel bowl. Add warm melted butter and whisk until well blended.

TO SERVE  Grease and sugar six 3-inch ramekins. Preheat the oven to 350°F. On each pastry round, spread 2 Tbsp of pastry cream. Cover the bottom of each ramekin with the rhubarb strips, cutting them to length so that they fit side by side. Place a pastry round on top, pastry cream–side down. Bake for about 20 minutes, until you see bubbles on the sides of the ramekins.

Remove ramekins from oven and flip rhubarb tarts out onto a serving plate. Place a piece of apple on top of each tart. Press a scoop of ice cream (about ⅓ cup) into a 2-inch ring mould and remove the ring. Place an ice cream round on top of the apple. Drizzle brown sugar sauce overtop and serve.

SUGGESTED WINE  Try an aged Passito di Pantelleria. Its apricot and orange spice flavours match the sweetness of the brown sugar sauce and are a great complement to the ginger ice cream.

# rha-barbarum

1 stalk rhubarb,
about 5 inches long, diced

1 tsp sugar

½ oz freshly squeezed lemon juice

1½ oz Maker's Mark bourbon

½ oz apricot liqueur

½ oz simple syrup (page 235)

2 dashes Angostura bitters

5 blueberries, skewered, for garnish

In this drink, rhubarb has a wonderful tartness that is complemented by the subtle honeyed sweetness of bourbon and a slightly bitter finish.

PLACE rhubarb into a mixing glass with sugar and lemon juice, then muddle to a pulp. Add bourbon, apricot liqueur, simple syrup and bitters. Fill the mixing glass with ice and shake vigorously until the shaker is very cold to the touch. If necessary, adjust the balance of sweetness and acidity to taste with additional simple syrup and lemon juice. Double-strain the cocktail into a chilled martini glass: using a cocktail strainer to hold back most of the pulp, strain through a tea strainer to remove the remaining fine pulp, tapping the strainer to help the liquid pass through.

Rest the skewered blueberries over the top of the cocktail and serve.

# jolicoeur

6-8 green grapes

2 oz Kim Crawford sauvignon blanc (or another New Zealand sauvignon blanc with tropical fruit notes)

1½ oz Grey Goose vodka

¾ oz elderberry flower syrup

¼ oz freshly squeezed lemon juice

1 small edible flower for garnish—you can find an assortment at a local specialty grocer

This cocktail is light, fresh and crisp, with floral notes. Because of the bright acidity and slight sweetness in this cocktail, it pairs well with goat cheese or light seafood dishes. This drink embodies the fun freshness of spring in the air and is a light enough tipple to quench a thirst. In the IKEA food market or at some specialty grocers you can find elderberry flower syrup, which will give the necessary sweetness to balance the cocktail and add a note of complexity.

MUDDLE grapes in a mixing glass. Add sauvignon blanc, vodka, elderberry syrup and lemon juice, then fill the mixing glass with ice. Shake vigorously until the shaker is very cold to the touch. If necessary, adjust the balance of sweetness and acidity to taste with additional elderberry syrup and lemon juice. Double-strain the cocktail into a chilled martini glass: using a cocktail strainer to hold back most of the pulp, strain through a tea strainer to remove the remaining fine pulp, tapping the strainer to help the liquid pass through.

# beet-nyk

BEET-INFUSED SYRUP

5 small organic yellow beets, stems and leaves discarded

15 oz water

15 oz simple syrup (page 235)

Juice of 2 lemons

BEET-NYK COCKTAIL

2 pieces of beet (from beet-infused syrup)

2 small sprigs dill

1 oz Luksusowa potato vodka

1¼ oz Giffard Manzana Verde or other apple liqueur

½ oz freshly squeezed lemon juice

1 oz beet-infused syrup

The beets in this cocktail have a wonderful natural sweetness that marries well with the fruity flavour of apples and the acidity of lemons, with the dill adding an interesting component to tie them all together. This is a fresh, lively and complex cocktail.

BEET-INFUSED SYRUP In a saucepan, cover the beets with water and boil until soft enough to easily insert a fork, 30 to 45 minutes depending on the size of the beets. Remove skin from beets with a paring knife and rinse with water to clean off any debris. Cut into 1-inch slices or pieces—usually with small beets this means quartering each beet—and place into a 4-cup jar. Add simple syrup and lemon juice, then fill the remaining portion of the jar with water. Cover the jar with its lid and allow the beets to infuse into the liquid for about 30 minutes in the refrigerator. The syrup will last for approximately one week in the refrigerator before natural fermentation begins. If you would like to have the beets last longer, change the syrup every 5 days, for a maximum of two changes, or add a neutral spirit like vodka at a ratio of 8 oz vodka per 4 cups of beet syrup; the alcohol prevents the fermentation from starting.

BEET-NYK COCKTAIL Place beet pieces into a mixing glass with one of the sprigs of dill, then muddle to a pulp. Add vodka, apple liqueur, lemon juice and beet-infused syrup. Fill the mixing glass with ice and shake vigorously until the shaker is very cold to the touch. If necessary, adjust the balance of sweetness and acidity to taste with additional beet-infused syrup and lemon juice. Double-strain the cocktail into a chilled martini glass: using a cocktail strainer to hold back most of the pulp, strain through a tea strainer to remove the remaining fine pulp, tapping the strainer to help the liquid pass through. Float the remaining sprig of dill on the surface of the cocktail and serve.

# bergamo

5 espresso beans

1 cube raw sugar

¼ blood orange, plus a small, round zest with pith removed for garnish

1 oz Appleton Reserve rum

1 oz Amaro Montenegro

2 dashes Fee Brothers orange bitters or another orange bitters

3 oz freshly squeezed orange juice

This drink offers a slight tartness from the blood orange, a touch of bitterness from the Amaro and natural sweetness from the orange, finished off nicely with a little hint of espresso flavour at the end.

COARSELY smash 4 espresso beans and sugar cube in a mixing glass with a muddling stick. Add blood orange and continue muddling. Add rum, Amaro, orange bitters and orange juice. Fill the mixing glass with ice and shake vigorously until the shaker is very cold to the touch. If necessary, adjust the balance of sweetness and acidity to taste with additional raw sugar and orange juice. Half-fill a chilled rock glass with ice, then double-strain the cocktail into it: using a cocktail strainer to hold back most of the pulp, strain through a tea strainer to remove the remaining fine pulp, tapping the strainer to help the liquid pass through. Float the blood orange zest, topped with an espresso bean, on the surface of the cocktail and serve.

summer

# a fine pairing

Owen Knowlton is wine director at West. He arrived circuitously, as is common in this business, from his home in Ontario through Banff, where he was the maître d'hotel and sommelier at the Rimrock Resort Hotel, followed by a stint as maître d' at Vancouver's Le Crocodile. He took over from Chris Van Nus, who had come to West from Araxi to become wine director. Chris's gifts in pairing food and wine set a high standard—one that Owen has met well and over time has built upon. The wine wall behind the bar, with its custom-built temperature-control system that allows less than one degree of temperature variance from bottom to top shelf, is not only impressive to see but also highly functional, and it stands as a symbol of West's commitment to wine and food as best enjoyed together.

"Ten years ago, our job was to show guests what to have," says Owen. "These days, we see all this knowledge on our guests' part, and our job is to help them explore—wine and food matches especially." West's approach is at once pragmatic and creative. "I taste the food and then develop pairings. It is not

about being 'book smart' but about balance and harmony," Owen notes. The ideal pairings are something elusive—magical if they can be found—and they can offer a diner a nirvanic moment or two.

But the norm, achievable but not straightforward, is to find wines that provide the right amount of body, aroma, weight, acidity, to function in effect as part of the dish they accompany. A pea-shoot risotto and oaked chardonnay might work against each other, but a good-quality Chablis, maybe even a 1er or grand cru, seems about right. "We consider the food first, then what our guests are prone to like. And if we don't know that, we are happy to have a discussion with them and see what they are interested in." Owen says, "We surround ourselves with educated staff. Everyone is passionate about the food, and the wine." Sommelier Corey Bauldry agrees: "At West it is about doing your best. You work hard, out of passion for it. It is a place to eat, but it has to be a comfortable place to eat, even with, maybe especially with, food of this quality." For Corey, "this restaurant is about finding the best ingredients and presenting them in the best way. In a sense, it is a humbling experience, a chef going through what is on the menu that evening and sharing them with you so that everyone can bring this to our guests in an informed, gracious way." Corey arrived at West after working at various restaurants and then on the demanding, hectic floor of Cioppino's.

The wine program, developing daily, reflects a commitment to finding the best combination of factors to create a unique fine-dining experience. According to Owen: "One of the most exciting aspects of the job is having guests pick your brain about the wine and food. People usually come here not only to eat but to have an experience well beyond everyday dinner," and wines are an integral part of West's offerings. Wine awareness continues to explode, along with a now overwhelming interest in organic, local, fresh foods. Biodynamic wine is becoming a hot topic as organic and sustainable practices in vineyards and wineries steadily increase worldwide.

Whether wines actually taste better if they are organic or biodynamic—the latter with its strict code of requirements including non-intervention, 100 per cent natural agricultural methods and complete sustainability—is still up for debate, but guests at West can engage in a full discussion on the topic with Owen, Corey and the servers if they wish. However, the team at West still considers being ready to provide a classical presentation—"here is the wine; here is why we are pouring it with this dish"—to be paramount. "I am big on atmosphere, certainly," says Owen. "But for me, it is always about the food. Then the wine, then the service. That is how a great dining experience is built, and all the elements have to be in place."

The food at West is, generally, light on sauces or heavy reductions. So pinot noir is in heavy demand, both by clients and by Owen himself. Some heavier whites, often chardonnays, find homes alongside West's dishes, although at West the New World style is sometimes a little out of sync with certain dishes, so French whites are important. New, exciting labels from around the world are on offer at West, although guests have also shown plenty of interest in local wines from British Columbia's Okanagan Valley. "There is a huge loyalty to local wines from the locals," says Owen, "but our out-of-town visitors, even international guests, are interested in trying the local wines as well. So that is an important part of our program." And, like other wine regions of the world, the Okanagan has its treasures; they are predictably difficult to source, but the experts at West unearth them to offer plenty of surprises, for locals and visitors alike.

# multicoloured beets baked on salt
## with warm marcella goat cheese

⅓ cup coarse sea salt

8 oz baby purple beets, washed and stalks trimmed

8 oz baby yellow beets, washed and stalks trimmed

8 oz baby candy cane beets, washed and stalks trimmed

1 rib celery, peeled and cut into twenty batons, each 2 inches long

2 oz watercress

4 cups sherry dressing (page 236)

5 oz Marcella goat cheese, cut into 4 rounds about ¾ inch thick

8 cherry tomatoes, quartered

10 candied walnuts (page 235)

12 celery leaves—the light green leaves from the heart of the celery

2 radishes, thinly sliced

1 apple, cored and sliced

*Serves 4*

Each variety of beet offers a subtle difference in flavour. Baking them in salt in this recipe allows them to get well and evenly seasoned. Marcella goat cheese is a firm and slightly sharp variety and is perfect for cooking.

PREHEAT the oven to 300°F.

Pour coarse salt into the middle of a large piece of aluminum foil (about 25 inches × 16 inches). Place the beets on top of the salt and wrap the foil tightly around the beets. Bake for 1 to 1½ hours. Allow to cool, then peel the beets and cut each one into quarters. Turn the broiler on.

Bring a small pot of salted water to a boil. Add celery batons and blanch for 1 minute, then plunge the celery into an ice bath to refresh.

In a small bowl, toss the watercress and celery in half of the sherry dressing. In a medium bowl, toss the beets with the remaining sherry dressing.

Quarter each round of cheese and place the segments on a baking sheet. Broil until cheese pieces are golden brown but still firm, about 45 seconds.

TO SERVE  Lay a quarter of the beets in a straight line on each of four plates. Sprinkle a quarter of the tomatoes, celery and watercress salad, walnuts, celery leaves, radish and apple overtop and top each dish with four pieces of warm goat cheese.

SUGGESTED WINE  Try a crisp, dry white with mineral notes and a high acidity to match the delightfully tart flavour of the goat cheese. Sauvignon blanc and goat cheese are a trendy pairing, and for good reason, since they work together fabulously. Chablis (not 1er or grand cru) or muscadet would also be nice pairings.

**GOAT CHEESE** was among many foods introduced to Europe by the Moors; Crottin de Chavignol (France), Castelo Branco (Portugal) and Caprino (Italy) are all reasonably well-known varieties. Goat cheese has evolved considerably from supermarket feta. That stalwart still has its place, but Salt Spring Island Cheese Company's David Wood has taken the humble chèvre into another dimension at West.

Like other cheeses, those made from goat milk come in all shapes, sizes and flavour profiles. Unlike cow milk, though, goat milk is more acidic (containing caproic, caprylic and capric acid, all from the Latin root *capra*, or goat) and thus tends to yield a somewhat tarter cheese. David Wood, who moved to Saltspring Island from a Toronto gourmet retail business in 1990, is the thoughtful, creative person who makes the cheese West reinvents on every plate. He notes that "goat milk is smoother and creamier than cow milk because of the tiny fat particles. They are so small they remain in suspension in the milk rather than rising to the surface. It results in a lovely texture and—if the feed is controlled properly—some wonderfully mild flavours which we can work with." From modest beginnings, David has built a growing business, but "it has been done very slowly. Making goat cheese is quite a lengthy process, when you take into account finding the animals you need and the fact that any increase in production cannot undermine the quality of what we produce." David Wood's dedication to perfection aligns well with the philosophy at West, where a goat cheese soup or goat cheese tortellini can clarify what using the best local ingredients actually means: freshness, texture and, above all, flavour.

# goat cheese

# goat cheese tortellini
# with artichoke barigoule

5 Tbsp olive oil

1 carrot, peeled and sliced

½ onion, sliced

2 cloves garlic

½ bulb fennel

4 medium artichokes, cleaned,
base and leaves trimmed

½ cup white wine

5 Tbsp white wine vinegar

½ cup chicken stock (page 231)

BARIGOULE SAUCE

7 Tbsp olive oil

2 cooked artichokes

Pinch of saffron

1 carrot, sliced thin with a mandolin

4 shallots, sliced into thin
rings with a mandolin

2 cloves garlic, sliced

1 sprig thyme, leaves picked
off and stems discarded

1 bay leaf

2 cups orange juice

⅓ cup artichoke cooking liquid
(from cooked artichokes)

4 basil leaves, julienned

Juice of 1 lemon

*Serves 4*

This dish works best with the freshest goat cheese you can find. This recipe calls for espelette pepper, which adds a very mild heat to a recipe—it is not hot but has a piquant after-bite that doesn't linger. You should be able to find it in most specialty food stores.

COOKED ARTICHOKES   In a large sauté pan, heat olive oil on medium heat. Add carrot, onion, garlic and fennel and sweat until softened and lightly golden, about 10 minutes. Add artichokes, then cover with wine, vinegar and stock and season with salt and pepper. Bring to a simmer and cook until soft, about 30 minutes.

BARIGOULE SAUCE   In a large sauté pan, heat 2 Tbsp of the olive oil. Add artichokes, saffron, carrot, shallots, garlic, thyme and bay leaf and sweat for 5 minutes until artichokes are soft but not browned. Deglaze the pan with orange juice, add artichoke cooking liquid and continue cooking until liquid is reduced by half, about 5 minutes. Finish with the remaining 5 Tbsp of olive oil.

## GOAT CHEESE TORTELLINI

8 oz fresh goat cheese

1 egg yolk

¼ cup whipping cream

Zest and juice of 1 lemon

Pinch of cayenne or
espelette pepper

1½ lbs pasta dough (page 237)

1¾ oz Parmesan cheese,
grated (about ⅔ cup)

GOAT CHEESE TORTELLINI  In a small mixing bowl, fold together goat cheese, egg yolk, whipping cream, lemon zest, lemon juice and cayenne or espelette pepper until well mixed.

Roll out the pasta dough to the thickness of a dime and cut into twelve discs 4 inches in diameter. Spoon about 1 cup of goat cheese filling into the middle of each disc, then fold the edges together and press to seal. Keep on a lightly floured board until ready to serve.

TO SERVE  Bring a large pot of salted water to a boil. Add tortellini and cook for 2 minutes or until soft.

Warm barigoule sauce and add basil and lemon juice. Add tortellini and toss to coat. Finish with Parmesan cheese. Divide among four bowls and serve immediately.

SUGGESTED WINE  A high-acid white is necessary for the artichokes. Try a quincy. It's made from the sauvignon blanc grape, and its herbal flavours pair nicely with the goat cheese as well. As an alternative, a Crémant de Loire goes very well with the dish, and the bubbles add a textural contrast to the goat cheese.

# terrine of foie gras, goat cheese and apple

⅓ cup white port

⅔ cup sweet wine,
like Essensia orange muscat

⅓ cup Armagnac

7 tsp sugar

7 tsp salt

½ tsp Chinese five-spice powder

2 lobes foie gras, about 1 lb each

8 oz Marcella goat cheese

¼ cup whipping cream

⅓ cup simple syrup (page 235)

2 Granny Smith apples,
peeled and finely sliced

1 celeriac, about 1 lb, peeled and
sliced dime-thin on a mandolin

½ cup apple juice

½ cup balsamic vinegar

¼ cup extra-virgin olive oil

*Serves 10+*

COMBINE white port, sweet wine, Armagnac, sugar, salt and five-spice powder in a marinating dish. Devein foie gras and add to the marinade. Cover and leave for 24 hours in the refrigerator.

Line a small terrine mould with plastic wrap and preheat the oven to 250°F. Press foie gras into the mould, cover with aluminum foil and place the mould in a baking dish. Pour boiling water into the baking dish around the terrine mould to make a bain marie, then place the baking dish in the oven and cook for 25 minutes. Remove the mould from the water, prick holes along the edge of the terrine and place a weight on top of the terrine to allow excess fat to escape. Leave the mould like this for 24 hours in the refrigerator.

Gently fold together goat cheese and cream.

Bring simple syrup to a boil in a small saucepan. Add apple slices, remove from heat and allow to cool.

Remove the foie gras from the terrine and slice into five equal pieces lengthwise. Reline the terrine mould with plastic wrap. Place the narrowest slice of foie gras in the terrine mould and cover with a single layer of sliced apple, followed by a ¼-inch thick layer of goat cheese and another layer of sliced apple. Place the next slice of foie gras on top and repeat the process. Pull the plastic wrap over the terrine, place a 2-lb weight on top and allow to set in the refrigerator.

Cut celeriac into discs 2 inches in diameter. Place in a small saucepan with the apple juice and balsamic vinegar. Cook on medium heat until the liquid is reduced to a syrup consistency, about 10 minutes. Season to taste with salt and pepper, then add the olive oil.

TO SERVE  On each of ten (or more) plates, arrange eight to ten slices of celeriac in a circle. Cut terrine into ½-inch slices, and place a slice of terrine in the middle of the plate.

SUGGESTED WINE  A rancio-style Rivesaltes is rich enough not to be overwhelmed by the foie gras, and its combination of fruit and aged character both complements and contrasts with the peppery sweet and sour notes in the balsamic syrup. Also, Tokaj Aszu 5 Puttonyos, a sweet wine from Hungary, is a treat when you can find it.

BELOW: terrine of foie gras, goat cheese and apple
RIGHT: tarte fine of porcini mushrooms with apple,
walnut and parsley dressing

# tarte fine of porcini mushrooms
# with apple, walnut and parsley dressing

PORCINI TARTE FINE

8 oz all-butter puff pastry

1 lb fresh porcini mushrooms

1½ Tbsp olive oil

3 Tbsp unsalted butter

½ onion, finely chopped

1 clove garlic, finely chopped

3 Tbsp Madeira

3 Tbsp whipping cream

¼ cup walnuts, chopped

1 oz dried porcini mushrooms

*Serves 4*

This recipe calls for preserved lemon and chardonnay vinegar, both available at specialty food stores. Preserved lemon is a whole lemon that has been packed in rock salt for four to six months then thoroughly washed. Just the skin is used, imparting a delicate lemon flavour to the dish. If you cannot find chardonnay vinegar, a relatively sweet white wine or cider vinegar would make a good substitute.

PORCINI TARTE FINE  Roll out puff pastry to ⅛ inch, dock with a fork and chill in the refrigerator for 1 hour.

Trim and set aside the stems from the fresh mushrooms. Cut the rest of the fresh mushrooms into ¼-inch slices. Heat olive oil and 2 Tbsp of the butter in a medium sauté pan on high heat. Add sliced mushrooms and brown for about 2 minutes on each side. Remove the mushrooms from the pan and lay them out on paper towels to drain.

Finely chop mushroom trimmings. Add onion and garlic to the hot pan and sweat for 2 to 3 minutes until onion is translucent. Add mushroom trimmings and cook until soft, about 4 minutes. Deglaze the pan with Madeira, then add cream and reduce for 10 to 12 minutes, or until the sauce has the consistency of porridge. Add walnuts and season this mushroom duxelle with salt and pepper.

Preheat the oven to 350°F. Spread mushroom duxelle evenly over the puff pastry, arrange sliced mushrooms on top and brush the top with the remaining 1 Tbsp of butter, melted first in the microwave.

DRESSING

4 tsp olive oil

1 tsp chardonnay vinegar

1 tsp lemon juice

2 tsp hazelnut oil

2 tsp honey

1 Granny Smith apple,
peeled and finely diced

2 oz walnuts, chopped
(about ¼ cup)

1 oz flat-leaf parsley, finely
chopped (about 3 Tbsp)

½ preserved lemon, finely diced

1 shallot, finely diced

Line a baking sheet with a silicone mat. Carefully invert the pastry onto the silicone and bake, mushroom-side down, for 18 minutes.

In a food processor or spice grinder, grind dried mushrooms to get a fine powder.

DRESSING  In a small bowl, whisk together olive oil, vinegar, lemon juice, hazelnut oil and honey to make a vinaigrette. Combine apple, walnuts, parsley, preserved lemon and shallot in a larger bowl, then add vinaigrette and toss to combine.

TO SERVE  Trim the edges of the pastry and cut into four pieces. Transfer each tarte fine to a plate, spoon dressing around the tart and dust with mushroom powder.

SUGGESTED WINE  Try Palo Cortado sherry. The earthiness of the mushrooms, the astringency of the walnuts and the sweetness of the apple in the dressing need a flexible wine to handle their contrasting flavours, and they find a true friend in this intense, full-bodied but dry sherry.

# tian of dungeness crab and couscous
# with smoked tomato gazpacho

CRAB AND COUSCOUS TIAN

16 cups court bouillon (page 229)

1 Dungeness crab (about 2 lbs)

1 cup couscous

¾ cup water

1/2 tsp saffron

½ red pepper, finely diced

Juice of 1 lime

Zest of 1 lime

2 Tbsp raisins, chopped

10 leaves cilantro, finely julienned

2 Tbsp mayonnaise (page 239)

1 tsp hummus (page 13)

Juice of 1 lemon

½ tsp basil oil (page 238)

*Serves 4*

CRAB AND COUSCOUS TIAN Bring court bouillon to a boil in a large pot on high heat. Add crab and cook for 8 minutes. Allow it to cool, crack the shells and pick out the crab meat. Reserve four nice-looking leg pieces for garnish.

Place uncooked couscous in a large heatproof bowl. Bring the water to a boil with saffron and a pinch of salt. The water will turn bright yellow. Pour this water over the couscous, gently stirring with a fork to get rid of any big lumps. Cover the bowl with plastic wrap and allow it to sit for 20 minutes. Set aside at room temperature.

Preheat the oven to 350°F. Place the red pepper in a roasting dish and roast it in the oven for about 20 minutes until brown. Peel off the skin and remove the seeds. Finely dice half of it, reserving the other half for the gazpacho or another recipe. Add the diced red pepper to the couscous, along with the lime juice, lime zest, raisins and cilantro.

Mix the crab meat with mayonnaise, hummus, lemon juice and salt.

Cut a 12-inch × 12-inch piece of plastic wrap. In the centre of the plastic wrap, spread a ¼-inch layer of couscous measuring about 6 inches × 3 inches. Spoon half of the crab mixture into the centre of the couscous rectangle. Using the plastic wrap, tightly roll the crab meat into the couscous, as if rolling sushi, to make a long cylinder about 1½ inches in diameter. Tie both ends of the plastic wrap and allow the cylinder to set in the refrigerator for at least 2 hours—any less time and the roll may fall apart. Cut another 12-inch × 12-inch piece of plastic wrap and repeat with the rest of the couscous and crab to make a second roll.

*Recipe continued overleaf. . .*

4 ripe Roma tomatoes

½ medium carrot

1 shallot

½ red pepper

1 clove garlic

2 Tbsp olive oil

¼ cucumber, peeled and cut into
½-inch cubes

3 basil leaves

Juice of 1 orange

½ tsp sugar

¼ tsp cumin seeds, toasted

¼ tsp paprika

1½ Tbsp sherry vinegar

1 bread roll, cut into ½-inch pieces

¼ cup tomato juice

SMOKED TOMATO GAZPACHO  Place the charcoal in the oven for 15 minutes to get it very hot. Remove it from the oven, then use a kitchen torch to ignite the charcoal and allow it to burn for 3 minutes. Place the charcoal in a solid stainless-steel pot. Sprinkle a handful of dry smoking wood chips on and around the charcoal. Place a perforated tray covered in aluminum foil 4 inches above the charcoal, then set the tomatoes on the foil, cover the pot and smoke for 5 minutes.

Preheat the oven to 350°F.

Toss carrot, shallot, red pepper and garlic in a roasting pan with the olive oil and roast for about 15 minutes until golden brown, stirring the vegetables halfway through.

Place the roasted vegetables, smoked tomatoes, cucumber, basil, orange juice, sugar, cumin, paprika, sherry vinegar and bread in a large non-reactive bowl. Cover with plastic wrap and refrigerate for 24 hours.

Transfer this mixture to a food processor. Add tomato juice and blend for 3 to 4 minutes, then pass it through a fine sieve and season with salt and pepper.

TO SERVE  In each of four soup bowls, ladle a quarter of the gazpacho. Unwrap the rolls and slice into 2-inch-tall tians, placing a tian in the centre of the gazpacho. Drizzle basil oil around the tian and top with a piece of crab leg meat.

SUGGESTED WINE  Rich, lush, concentrated whites like good Alsace pinot gris or muscat and viognier from Australia are best.

TO SERVE  In the centre of each of four round plates, spoon about 2 tsp of purée. Using the back of the spoon, gently swirl the purée outward to form a circle about 3 inches in diameter.

Spoon a quarter of the tartare mix into a 2½-inch ring mould and press down with the back of the spoon. Transfer the mould and the tartare to one of the plates and place them in the centre of the purée. Remove the ring mould and place a roasted tomato disc on top of the tartare.

Sprinkle tomatoes concassé and fried cilantro around tartare. Arrange three prawns around the purée, then drizzle the dressing around. Rest the tuile of crispy fish skin against the tartare.

SUGGESTED WINE  This dish calls for something light and stimulating, The bubbles of Champagne or a good B.C. sparkling wine would cool and clean the palate of any heat from the ginger, making every bite new and fresh. Many white wines would work with this dish, but avoid red wine and heavily oaked chardonnays.

# white velouté of vine-ripened
# tomato and marcella goat cheese

10 very ripe Roma tomatoes

1 large leek, white part only, chopped

1 clove garlic, crushed

3 green onions, chopped

4 ribs celery, chopped

2 sprigs thyme, leaves picked
off and stems discarded

2 oz basil, julienned (about 6 Tbsp)

4 cups tomato juice

⅓ cup sugar

⅓ cup whipping cream

4 oz Marcella goat cheese

2 egg yolks

4 tomatoes concassé (page 237)

Basil oil for garnish (page 238)

*Serves 4*

COMBINE tomatoes, leek, garlic, green onions, celery, thyme, 1 oz of the basil, tomato juice and sugar in a blender and purée until smooth. Transfer to a medium saucepan and bring to a simmer. Remove from heat as soon as the soup comes to a light boil. Allow to cool, strain through a cheesecloth-lined sieve, then chill overnight in the refrigerator.

Whisk together cream, goat cheese and egg yolks to make a liaison. Warm the tomato mixture on low heat until it is heated through, then whisk in the liaison. The soup should have the consistency of cream. Season with salt and pepper.

TO SERVE Ladle soup into four bowls. Garnish each bowl with a quarter of the tomatoes concassé, ¼ oz of basil and a drizzle of basil oil.

SUGGESTED WINE Try a good-quality (unoaked) B.C. pinot blanc or pinot gris, or Italian pinot grigio from the Veneto or Friuli. The ripe pear and apple fruit qualities of these wines, along with their crisp acidities, harmonize well with the tomatoes in this soup, and their minerally, smoky finishes will complement the goat cheese nicely.

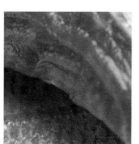

**RESPECT FOR** the food on your plate is something of a mantra for chefs. When you consider the potential thousand-mile migration for sockeye salmon, that respect is perhaps a little easier to give. The cycle of a salmon finding gravel redds in which to lay eggs, those eggs hatching, the fry taking a trip downstream to the ocean, and each grown fish embarking on a spawning trek back to the exact redd that was its birthplace is well documented. Finest at Sea Ocean Products operates a small troller fleet and line-catches salmon in the cold waters off the west side of Vancouver Island. The fish are frozen at sea: the fishers quickly clean and bleed the fish, then immediately "glaze" them—by rapid submersion in ice-cold sea water—to create an icy sheath around the entire fish. It is then flash-frozen, a process that takes seconds rather than minutes.

The result is a fish that arrives at West in virtually identical condition to what it would be had you caught, cleaned and prepared to cook it right on the shore of the waters it swam in. The spawning runs begin in June and can last until September. Summer, then, is the time to enjoy fresh salmon. Five species of salmon populate Pacific coastal waters: sockeye, chinook (also commonly known as spring), coho, chum and pink. Size is usually the more reliable indicator of flavour than is colour: the bigger, the better. Colour is dependent on diet, and the more shrimp and prawns the fish eats, the darker its flesh becomes. Sockeye, prized for their high fat content and resultant rich flavour, can actually resemble, in texture and to a surprising degree in taste, a fine piece of rib-eye steak. The fish's journey to your plate is arduous; appreciating it will be anything but.

# salmon

confit fillet of sockeye salmon with tomato-
red pepper compote and goat cheese ravioli

# confit fillet of sockeye salmon with tomato-red pepper compote and goat cheese ravioli

## TOMATO–RED PEPPER COMPOTE

2 red peppers

1 Tbsp olive oil

2 banana shallots, finely chopped

1 clove garlic, finely chopped

8 tomatoes concassé (page 237)

1 sprig thyme

1 bay leaf

¼ cup white wine

⅓ cup tomato juice

1 oz parsley, chopped (about 3 Tbsp)

## GOAT CHEESE RAVIOLI

4 oz soft, young goat cheese

5 tsp whipping cream

Skin of 1 preserved lemon, julienned

5 oz pasta dough (page 237)

1 egg

1 egg yolk

¼ cup unsalted butter

¼ cup water

*Serves 4*

For this recipe you will need banana shallots, which are available at specialty food stores.

TOMATO AND RED PEPPER COMPOTE  Preheat the oven to 350°F.

Roll peppers in 2 tsp of the olive oil. Season with salt, then place in the oven for 25 to 30 minutes until the peppers are soft. Remove them from the oven and place in a bowl. Cover the bowl with plastic wrap and allow to rest for about 30 minutes. Remove the skin and seeds from the red pepper and roughly dice the flesh.

In a small sauté pan, heat the remaining olive oil on medium heat. Add shallots and garlic and sweat until soft, about 2 minutes, being careful not to burn the shallots. Add tomatoes concassé, red pepper flesh, thyme and bay leaf and cook gently for 2 to 3 minutes. Add wine, cook until nearly all of the liquid has evaporated, then add tomato juice and cook until all of the liquid has evaporated. Remove from heat, discard the thyme and bay leaf, season with salt and pepper, and add parsley.

GOAT CHEESE RAVIOLI  In a small bowl, fold together goat cheese and cream, then fold in half of the lemon skin. Put this mixture into a piping bag with a ½-inch nozzle.

Roll out pasta dough in two sheets about 4 inches wide and the thickness of a dime, or use the lowest setting on a pasta machine. Along the centre line of one of the sheets, pipe the goat cheese mixture in twelve 1-inch-diameter rounds about 1½ inches apart.

In a small bowl, beat together the egg, egg yolk and a pinch of salt to make an egg wash. Brush the edges of the pasta and between the fillings with egg

CONFIT SALMON

2 cups duck fat

4 fillets sockeye salmon,
4 to 5 oz each

2 tsp olive oil

4 oz baby spinach

8 sprigs cress leaves,
for garnish

wash and cover with the second sheet of pasta. Press to seal the pasta dough between the fillings and along the edges and cut out individual ravioli.

In a small saucepan, melt butter along with the water on low heat. Add the remaining preserved lemon skin. Season to taste with salt and pepper.

CONFIT SALMON In a large sauté pan, heat duck fat no hotter than 150°F— use a thermometer to confirm temperature. Gently place salmon into the fat and cook for 7 to 9 minutes, until salmon is firm but still somewhat translucent. It is important that the salmon be pink inside and not be leaking white protein. Remove the fish from the fat and drain on paper towels. Allow to rest for 2 to 3 minutes.

Heat olive oil in a small sauté pan on high heat. Add spinach and sauté for 30 seconds.

TO SERVE Bring a large pot of salted water to a boil. Add ravioli and cook for 3 to 4 minutes. Remove from the water and toss in the lemon-butter emulsion.

At the centre of each of four plates, heap a quarter of the compote and top with a fillet of salmon. Arrange three ravioli around the fish and spoon some of the lemon-butter emulsion overtop. Garnish with two sprigs of cress per plate.

SUGGESTED WINE The weight of a dry chenin blanc from Savennières goes well with the salmon, and its high acidity pairs well with the tomatoes and goat cheese. If you would like to try local, B.C. pinot gris and salmon are delicious together and hard to beat. South African chenin blanc, also known as steen, would work well, too.

# supreme of wild salmon with sesame-scented cabbage and smoked salmon gnocchi

## SMOKED SALMON GNOCCHI

½ cup unsalted butter

½ cup flour, plus extra for dredging

1 cup milk

5 oz smoked salmon, diced and frozen

4 cups vegetable oil for deep frying

## SMOKED SALMON CREAM

⅔ cup smoked salmon stock (page 230)

¼ cup whipping cream

4 tsp cold unsalted butter

½ lemon

*Serves 4*

Ask your fishmonger for larger cuts off the salmon fillet for this dish.

SMOKED SALMON GNOCCHI  In a small saucepan, heat butter on medium heat. Add flour and stir well to combine. Slowly add milk to form a paste. Refrigerate this Béchamel for 2 hours until cold.

In a food processor, blend together Béchamel and frozen smoked salmon into a smooth paste. Pass this mixture through a fine sieve, then roll it into a ¼-inch-diameter cylinder. Cut the cylinder into ¾-inch pieces to make gnocchi.

Bring a medium pot of water to a boil. Add smoked salmon gnocchi and blanch for 1 minute. Plunge them into an ice bath to refresh, then drain them.

Heat oil in a deep fryer or a deep pot to 350°F. Gently toss salmon gnocchi in flour to coat, then fry them in the oil for 30 seconds. Remove the gnocchi from the oil and allow them to drain on paper towels.

SMOKED SALMON CREAM  In a small saucepan, heat salmon stock on medium heat until reduced to a glaze, about 20 minutes. Add cream and bring to a boil, then whisk in cold butter, salt, pepper and a squeeze of lemon juice.

RAISIN PURÉE  In a medium saucepan, combine raisins, sweet wine, water and five-spice powder. Bring to a boil, then allow to simmer for 5 minutes. Remove 4 tsp of raisins and set them aside. In a blender, purée the rest of the raisin mixture until smooth and pass through a fine sieve.

⅔ cup golden raisins

¼ cup sweet wine,
like Essensia orange muscat

⅓ cup water

Pinch of Chinese five-spice powder

SESAME-SCENTED CABBAGE
AND SUPREME OF SALMON

4 tsp olive oil

8 oz white cabbage, finely sliced

4 tsp raisins (reserved
from raisin purée)

2 tsp toasted sesame oil

1 oz parsley, julienned (about 3 Tbsp)

4 fillets wild salmon, 5 oz each

Deep-fried parsley for
garnish (page 237)

SESAME-SCENTED CABBAGE AND SUPREME OF SALMON Heat a large, heavy-bottomed saucepan on high heat. Add 2 tsp of the olive oil and cabbage and stir vigorously for 3 to 4 minutes. Add raisins and sesame oil, then season with salt and pepper. Remove from heat and finish with fresh parsley.

Preheat the oven to 350°F.

Heat 1 tsp olive oil in a large ovenproof sauté pan on high heat. Add salmon, skin-side down. Place in the oven and roast for 3 to 4 minutes. Remove the salmon from oven, turn the fillets over, then season with salt and pepper and brush with the remaining 1 tsp of olive oil.

TO SERVE Spoon 2 tsp of the raisin purée around each of four plates. Place a quarter of the sesame-scented cabbage in the middle and top with a supreme of salmon. Sprinkle a quarter of the gnocchi around each plate, then spoon 2 tsp of the smoked salmon cream overtop. Garnish with fried parsley.

SUGGESTED WINE Pinot grigio from the Trentino-Alto Adige in the northeast of Italy makes a beautiful pairing with this dish. It has aromas of peach and pear, and in the mouth it delivers nuances of stone fruit and honey that complement the sweetened cabbage. The higher alcohol of pinot grigio gives it the power to balance the fatty oils of the salmon.

# seared, then braised, wild salmon
# with twelve vegetables

4 fillets wild spring salmon,
5 oz each

2 Tbsp extra-virgin olive oil

8 green beans, finely sliced

16 small florets cauliflower
(about 3 oz)

8 small chanterelle
mushrooms, halved

8 baby carrots

4 baby turnips, quartered

8 sugar snap peas, halved

3¾ cups vegetable stock (page 228)

⅓ cup English peas pods removed

1 baby zucchini,
sliced into eight pieces

16 fava beans

½ cup baby spinach

½ cup sweet corn kernels

3 Tbsp cold unsalted butter,
cut into ¼-inch cubes

12 cherry tomatoes, halved

½ oz chives, chopped (about 1 Tbsp)

½ oz tarragon, chopped
(about 1 Tbsp)

Juice of 1 lemon

*Serves 4*

SEASON the salmon with kosher salt. Heat oil in a large pan and sear the fillets for 1 minute per side. Remove from the pan.

To the pan, add green beans, cauliflower, chanterelles, carrots, turnips and sugar snap peas. Cook for 1 minute. Cover with vegetable stock, add salmon fillets back to the pan and bring to a simmer. Cook for 4 to 5 minutes.

Add English peas, zucchini and fava beans, and cook for 1 minute more.

Add baby spinach and sweet corn. Remove the salmon fillets and set aside.

Whisk butter into vegetable mixture. Once butter has emulsified, add cherry tomatoes, chives and tarragon. Season with salt and lemon juice to taste.

TO SERVE  In the middle of each of four bowls, ladle a quarter of the vegetables and broth and place a salmon fillet overtop.

SUGGESTED WINE  Try a medium- to full-dry white with floral and mineral notes, perhaps 1er Chablis, roussane or viognier.

# halibut braised over mushrooms

4 tsp unsalted butter

3 shallots, sliced

1 sprig thyme

1 bay leaf

10 button mushrooms, sliced

⅓ cup Noilly Prat or a dry white wine

⅓ cup fish stock (page 229)

4 halibut fillets,
5 oz each (centre cut)

5 tsp whipping cream

Juice of 1 lemon

½ oz chives, chopped
(about 1 Tbsp)

*Serves 4*

This dish is a great way to serve any white fish and is best accompanied with fresh asparagus, chanterelles and peas.

PREHEAT the oven to 375°F.

In a large, ovenproof sauté pan, heat the butter on medium heat. Add shallots, along with thyme and bay leaf, and sauté until soft but not brown, about 10 minutes. Add mushrooms and cook for another 3 minutes. Add Noilly Prat (or dry white wine), then cook until liquid is reduced to a syrup, about 5 minutes. Add fish stock and reduce by half, about 8 minutes.

Add halibut fillets on top of the mushroom and shallot mixture. When the liquid has come back to a simmer, place the pan into the oven and cook for 9 minutes.

Remove the fish from the liquid and heat the pan on the stove at medium heat until the remaining liquid is reduced by half, about 8 minutes. Stir in whipping cream. Bring back to a simmer, then strain this sauce through a fine sieve. Season with lemon juice and salt, and finish with chives.

TO SERVE Place a fish fillet into the middle of each of four bowls and gently pour the sauce overtop.

SUGGESTED WINE Your finest dry white, like a Chassagne Montrachet or Condrieu, would work well with this dish.

# fillet of mackerel with cannelloni
# of smoked eggplant and pine nuts

## TOMATO–SHALLOT SAUCE

6 Roma tomatoes,
halved and seeded

3 shallots, halved

1 clove garlic, finely sliced

Pinch of rock salt

1 Tbsp olive oil

1 oz parsley, chopped
(about ¼ cup)

## CANNELLONI

1 eggplant, about 7 oz

2 tomatoes concassé (page 237)

1 oz pine nuts, toasted

1 tsp tahini

1 sprig thyme, leaves picked
off and stem discarded

4 oz pasta dough (page 237)

2 tsp olive oil

*Serves 4*

TOMATO–SHALLOT SAUCE Preheat the oven to 300°F. Place tomatoes, shallots, garlic and rock salt onto a sheet of aluminum foil 12 inches × 12 inches. Drizzle with olive oil, then fold the foil over the mixture and seal into a packet. Place the packet onto a baking sheet and cook in the oven for 4 to 5 hours.

Remove the packet from the oven, extract its contents, discard the shallot and tomato skins, then roughly run a knife through the tomato mixture to make a coarse purée. Add parsley and season with salt and pepper.

CANNELLONI Place eggplant on an open-flame burner and turn it every 3 or 4 minutes until the outside is entirely charred. Cut it in half, spoon out and discard the seeds, then spoon out the flesh. Finely chop the flesh and allow it to drain in a sieve, then place it in a medium bowl. Add tomatoes concassé, pine nuts, tahini and thyme and season with salt and pepper. Transfer this eggplant mixture into a piping bag with a ½-inch nozzle.

Roll out pasta dough to the thickness of a dime. Bring a large pot of salted water to a boil. Add pasta and blanch for 2 minutes, then remove it from the pot and plunge it into an ice bath to refresh.

Cut the pasta into eight 4-inch × 8-inch rectangles. Pipe a line of the eggplant mixture along one of the 8-inch edges of each pasta rectangle. Roll the pasta over the filling into a cigar shape and wrap each cannellono in plastic wrap. Leave in the refrigerator to set overnight.

Remove the plastic wrap from the cannelloni. Trim the ends off each cannellono, then cut each cannellono in half. Heat olive oil in a non-stick sauté pan on medium heat. Add the cannelloni and gently fry for about 1 minute per side until golden, starting with the side of the seam.
*Recipe continued overleaf. . .*

5 oz flat-leaf parsley, leaves
picked off and stems discarded

¼ cup olive oil

2 tsp white wine vinegar

lemon juice to taste

PAN-FRIED MACKEREL

4 tsp olive oil

2 mackerel, 1 lb each,
filleted and pin bones removed

Deep-fried parsley for
garnish (page 237)

Preheat the oven to 350°F. When the cannelloni are brown, transfer them, seam-side down, to a baking dish and bake in the oven for 4 to 5 minutes.

PARSLEY VINAIGRETTE  Bring a small pot of water to a boil. Add parsley leaves and blanch until leaves begin to dissolve, about 3 minutes, then plunge them into an ice bath to refresh. In a blender, combine parsley, olive oil and vinegar, and blend until smooth. Season this vinaigrette with salt, pepper and lemon juice.

PAN-FRIED MACKEREL  Heat oil in a large, non-stick sauté pan on high heat, then add the mackerel fillets, skin-side down, and fry for 3 to 4 minutes. Turn the fish over, remove the pan from heat and season with salt and pepper.

TO SERVE  Place a quarter of the tomato-shallot sauce into the centre of each of four plates. Place two cannelloni on top, then top with a mackerel fillet. Spoon 2 tsp of vinaigrette overtop and garnish with fried parsley.

SUGGESTED WINE  The dry, crisp whites of Sancerre or Touraine deliver a more mineral and herb characteristic, which works best for this dish. The clean, refreshing style of the fashionable albariño from Rías Baixas works well also.

# baked canadian sturgeon with
# velouté of saffron, mussels and bacon

## VELOUTÉ

4 tsp olive oil

1 onion, roughly chopped

1 bulb fennel, roughly chopped

1 clove garlic, roughly chopped

2 oz dry-cured bacon, diced,
with trimmings reserved

3 lbs mussels,
washed and debearded

Pinch of saffron

¼ cup white wine

⅓ cup whipping cream

⅓ cup chicken stock (page 231)

2 tsp cold unsalted butter

## HERBED BREAD CRUMBS

1 cup fresh bread crumbs

1 oz parsley (about 3 Tbsp)

1 oz chervil (about 3 Tbsp)

1 oz tarragon (about 3 Tbsp)

1 oz dill (about 3 Tbsp)

⅓ oz thyme leaves (about 1½ Tbsp)

## BAKED STURGEON

2 zucchinis, 8 oz each

5 tsp olive oil + extra for garnish

4 fillets sturgeon, 5 oz each

*Serves 4*

VELOUTÉ  In a heavy-bottomed pot, heat olive oil on high heat. Add onion, fennel and garlic and cook for 3 to 4 minutes until soft. Add bacon trimmings, then add mussels, saffron and wine. Cover and cook until all the mussels are open, about 3 minutes. Strain through a colander, reserving the liquid. Discard the mussel shells, but keep all of the mussel flesh and the vegetables. Pick out 25 to 30 nice-looking mussels and set them aside.

Pour the liquid back into the pan, add cream and bring to a boil. Add mussels and vegetables and simmer for 4 to 5 minutes (add chicken stock if the liquid has evaporated before the vegetables are soft). Purée this soup in a blender and pass it through a fine sieve. Season with salt and pepper.

In a small sauté pan on high heat, sauté the diced bacon for 3 minutes until golden. Add reserved mussels and heat gently for 2 minutes.

HERBED BREAD CRUMBS  Put bread crumbs into a food processor. Add parsley, chervil, tarragon, dill, thyme, salt and pepper and blend until fine.

BAKED STURGEON  Grate zucchinis with a cheese grater, season with salt, leave for 2 minutes, then drain. In a small sauté pan, heat 2 tsp of the olive oil on high heat, then add zucchini and cook 1 minute until just wilted.

Preheat the oven to 350°F. In a large sauté pan, heat another 2 tsp of the olive oil on high heat. Add sturgeon and sear on each side for 2 minutes until caramelized. Transfer sturgeon to a baking sheet, drizzle with the remaining 1 tsp of olive oil, season with salt and pepper, and bake for 6 to 7 minutes. Remove from heat and allow to rest for 3 to 4 minutes.

TO SERVE  Bring velouté to a simmer, whisk in cold butter, then add the mussels and bacon. In each of four bowls, arrange zucchini strands in a nest. Place a portion of sturgeon on top and pour a quarter of the velouté around. Garnish with the bread crumbs and a drizzle of olive oil.

SUGGESTED WINE  Try a Burgundy like Chassagne-Montrachet or St.-Aubin.

# blue cheese cake with port-braised blueberries and cinnamon brioche toast

**BLUE CHEESE CAKE**

2½ oz blue cheese

9 oz cream cheese

⅓ cup sugar

3 eggs

4½ Tbsp whipping cream

**PORT-BRAISED BLUEBERRIES**

½ cup port

½ vanilla bean, split and scraped, but pod reserved

½ cup brown sugar

1 lb blueberries

**BRIOCHE**

4 eggs

¼ cup whole milk

1½ cups flour

1½ tsp salt

1 Tbsp yeast

1 cup unsalted butter, warmed to room temperature

**CINNAMON BRIOCHE TOAST**

6 slices brioche, each ¾ inch thick

⅓ cup sugar

4 tsp cinnamon

½ cup unsalted butter, melted

*Serves 6*

Brioche is a rich, buttery bread that is tender to slice. Any excess brioche can be frozen and used later. Use a sharp, creamy blue cheese for this recipe—Stilton would work quite well. This recipe calls for timbale cups, which are drum-shaped metal moulds, available at kitchen supply stores. If you do not have them, ramekins will work just as well.

BLUE CHEESE CAKE  In the bowl of an electric mixer with paddle attachment, cream together blue cheese, cream cheese and sugar. Add eggs, one at a time, scraping down the sides of the bowl after each addition to avoid lumps. Add cream and mix until well blended.

Preheat the oven to 325°F.

Grease and sugar six 4-oz timbale cups. Fill cups with the cream cheese mixture and place into a roasting pan. Pour water into the roasting pan until the water level reaches halfway up the cups. Cover the pan with aluminum foil and bake for about 40 minutes, or until the batter has slightly souffléed and a toothpick inserted into the centre of each cake comes out clean. Allow to cool and refrigerate for 2 hours.

PORT-BRAISED BLUEBERRIES  In a medium saucepan, combine port, vanilla bean (both seeds and pod) and brown sugar. Simmer on medium heat until reduced to the consistency of honey, about 10 minutes. Add blueberries and stir until berries are heated through, about 5 minutes. Allow to cool, then remove and discard the vanilla pod.

BRIOCHE  In the bowl of an electric mixer with paddle attachment, combine eggs, milk, flour, salt and yeast and mix to form a smooth dough. Add butter, about ¼ cup at a time, scraping down the sides of the bowl after each addition. The dough should be very soft, smooth and elastic.

*Recipe continued overleaf. . .*

Chill in the refrigerator for 8 to 12 hours or overnight.

Grease an 8-inch × 4-inch loaf pan. On a floured surface, roll the dough into a cylinder and press evenly into the loaf pan. Spray the top of the dough with cooking spray to keep it from drying out. Allow to proof, uncovered, in a warm area until dough almost doubles in volume, 1 or 2 hours.

Preheat the oven to 400°F.

Bake brioche loaf until golden brown, about 40 minutes. Unmould the loaf and return it to the oven for about 10 minutes. Allow to cool on a wire rack.

CINNAMON BRIOCHE TOAST  Preheat the oven to 375°F.

Using a cutter 2½ inches in diameter, cut rounds from the brioche slices. Combine sugar and cinnamon in a shallow dish. Brush the brioche rounds with melted butter, then toss the rounds in the cinnamon sugar. Place on a baking sheet and bake for about 8 minutes. Turn each slice over and bake another 8 minutes, or until lightly toasted.

TO SERVE  Unmould the blue cheese cake and smooth the edges with a palette knife dipped in hot water. On each of six plates, place a slice of brioche toast. Top with a blue cheese cake. Pile a sixth of the blueberries on top of and around the cake, then drizzle the port reduction overtop.

SUGGESTED WINE  Although this suggestion is rather specific, the Brandenburg No. 3 from Venturi-Schulze on Vancouver Island has the richness and the acidity to stand up to the blue cheese, and its oxidative plum and spice flavours are great with the blueberry compote. A ten-year-old tawny port would be fine as well.

# freestone peaches poached in moscato d'asti with frangipane and blackberry coulis

POACHED PEACHES

1½ cups Moscato d'Asti

½ cup sugar

½ vanilla bean, split and scraped, but pod reserved

2 ripe freestone peaches

FRANGIPANE

⅓ cup unsalted butter

½ cup sugar

⅓ cup almond paste

Zest of 1 lemon

1 tsp vanilla extract

2 eggs

⅓ cup flour

1 cup ground almonds

BLACKBERRY COULIS

1¼ cups blackberries

⅓ cup sugar syrup (page 235)

*Serves 4*

This dessert calls for almond paste, which is available at specialty food stores.

POACHED PEACHES  In a medium saucepan, heat Moscato d'Asti, sugar and vanilla bean (both seeds and pod) on medium heat until sugar is dissolved. Rub the fuzz off the peaches with a damp cloth. Cut each peach in half and remove pits. Add to syrup and simmer until peaches are heated through, about 40 minutes. Allow to cool. Remove the peach skins.

FRANGIPANE  Preheat the oven to 350°F.

In the bowl of an electric mixer with paddle attachment, combine butter, sugar, almond paste, lemon zest and vanilla until light and fluffy. Continue mixing while adding eggs one at a time. Add flour and ground almonds. Scrape down the sides of the bowl and continue mixing until the dough is smooth.

Spread dough evenly onto an 8-inch square pan and bake until golden, about 30 minutes. Allow to cool and cut into four rounds the same width as the peach halves.

BLACKBERRY COULIS  Purée blackberries in a blender, then strain through a fine sieve into a small bowl, discarding the solids. Mix in sugar syrup.

TO SERVE  Spoon a quarter of the blackberry coulis onto each of four plates. Place a round of frangipane in the centre of each plate. Top the frangipane with half a peach, cut-side down.

SUGGESTED WINE  Canadian late-harvest botrytis-affected optima is great with the gently sweet peach and blackberry flavours of this dessert and holds on with the frangipane as well. A Moscato d'Asti—the wine the peach is poached in—is a natural for this dish, too.

# marsala-roasted fig with almond custard, vanilla ice cream and oat tuile

### ALMOND CUSTARD

⅔ cup ground almonds

½ cup icing sugar

4 eggs

½ tsp vanilla extract

1 Tbsp flour

½ tsp salt

1 cup whipping cream

⅓ cup whole milk

¼ cup unsalted butter, melted

### VANILLA ICE CREAM

8 egg yolks

1 cup sugar

1 cup whole milk

1 cup whipping cream

½ vanilla bean, split and scraped, but pod reserved

*Serves 6*

ALMOND CUSTARD  Line an 8-inch square cake pan with parchment paper and preheat the oven to 350°F.

Whisk together ground almonds, icing sugar, eggs, vanilla, flour, salt, cream and milk until smooth. Add warm melted butter. Pour into the cake pan and bake for about 20 minutes, or until the top is lightly golden and a toothpick stuck into the centre comes out clean. Allow to cool and cut into 2-inch rounds.

VANILLA ICE CREAM  In a large heatproof mixing bowl, whisk together egg yolks and sugar until the mixture turns a pale yellow. In a medium saucepan, bring milk, cream and vanilla bean (both seeds and pod) to a boil. Slowly pour hot milk mixture into the egg yolks while whisking vigorously. Return this custard to the saucepan and cook on high heat, stirring constantly until the mixture coats the back of a spoon. Allow to cool, remove and discard the vanilla pod, then pour custard into an ice cream machine and process according to the manufacturer's instructions.

OAT TUILE  Preheat the oven to 350°F and line a baking sheet with a silicone mat or parchment paper.

In the bowl of an electric mixer, cream together butter and sugar until light and fluffy. Add vanilla and egg whites and continue mixing, making sure to scrape down the sides of the bowl. Add oats, flour and cinnamon and mix until well incorporated.

Spread a thin layer of batter across a 2½-inch round template onto the lined baking sheet. Remove the template, leaving a round disc of batter. Repeat until you have made six tuiles.

½ cup unsalted butter

½ cup sugar

1 tsp vanilla extract

⅔ cup egg whites (about 5 eggs)

¾ cup ground oats

½ cup flour

½ tsp cinnamon

MARSALA-ROASTED FIGS

6 large, ripe figs

¼ cup unsalted butter

½ cup sugar

1 cup Marsala

⅓ cup water

Bake until golden brown, about 8 minutes. Allow to cool. Tuiles may be made up to 2 weeks in advance and stored in an airtight container until needed.

MARSALA-ROASTED FIGS Preheat the oven to 350°F.

Slice about a quarter off the tops of the figs, and place figs into a small roasting pan. Dot the top of each fig with about 1 tsp of the butter. Sprinkle with sugar. Add ⅔ cup of the Marsala and the fig tops to the pan. Roast until pink juices appear and figs are heated through. Remove the figs from the pan and set aside. Deglaze the pan with the remaining ⅓ cup of Marsala and the water and pour the liquid into a small saucepan. Heat Marsala sauce on high heat until reduced to the consistency of honey, about 5 minutes. Remove from heat and whisk in the remaining 2 Tbsp of butter.

TO SERVE On each of six plates, place a custard round in the centre. Top with a fig, then drizzle the fig with Marsala sauce. Place an oat tuile on the fig. Use a small ice cream scoop or a melon-baller dipped in hot water to place a scoop of ice cream on top.

SUGGESTED WINE The Tuscan vin santo's oxidative fruit flavours go well with the Marsala-roasted fig, and the almond flavours in the custard draw a latent nutty quality out of the wine. Madeira makes a great match as well—for a special treat (the wine is dear), splurge on a bottle of Bual Madeira, the royal cousin of the Marsala the fig is roasted with.

# fresh raspberries with lemon tuiles, cream cheese ice cream and nobo fruit tea syrup

### LEMON TUILES

½ cup unsalted butter

1 cup sugar

½ cup egg whites
(about 4 large eggs)

1 tsp vanilla extract

1 tsp lemon reduction (page 236)

Zest of 1 lemon

1 cup flour

4 cups fresh raspberries

### CREAM CHEESE ICE CREAM

½ cup whipping cream

½ cup whole milk

¼ vanilla bean, split and
scraped, but pod reserved

2 Tbsp honey

3 egg yolks

⅓ cup sugar

2½ oz cream cheese
(about ⅓ cup)

*Serves 6*

Nobo fruit tea is a tea made up of dried berries, hibiscus, apple and rosehips. Together with sugar it makes a rich, fruity-flavoured syrup. Ask for it at your local tea shop.

LEMON TUILES  Preheat the oven to 350°F and line a baking sheet with a silicone mat or parchment paper.

In the bowl of an electric mixer, cream together butter and sugar using the paddle attachment until the mixture is fluffy and pale yellow. Gradually add egg whites, vanilla, lemon reduction and lemon zest, occasionally scraping the sides of the bowl to make sure that the ingredients are fully incorporated. Add flour, then scrape the sides of the bowl again.

Using an offset spatula and a round template 3 inches in diameter, spread a thin layer of batter across the template onto the lined baking sheet. Remove the template to leave a disc of batter. Repeat until you have made twelve tuiles.

Bake in the oven for 6 minutes or until golden brown.

CREAM CHEESE ICE CREAM  In a medium saucepan, bring cream, milk, vanilla bean (both seeds and pod) and honey to a boil.

Meanwhile, whisk together egg yolks and sugar in a medium heatproof mixing bowl.

Slowly add the hot cream mixture to the egg yolks, whisking constantly. Return this custard to the saucepan and cook on high heat, stirring constantly, until the mixture coats the back of a spoon. Remove and discard the vanilla pod, then whisk in cream cheese.

Remove from heat and cool over an ice bath. Strain through a fine sieve. Pour into an electric ice cream machine and process according to the manufacturer's instructions.

*Recipe continued overleaf. . .*

NOBO FRUIT TEA SYRUP

1 cup water

½ cup dried nobo fruit tea

½ cinnamon stick

½ vanilla pod, split and
scraped, but pod reserved

½ cup sugar

Juice of 1 lemon

NOBO FRUIT TEA SYRUP  In a small saucepan, simmer water, tea, cinnamon and vanilla for about 10 minutes. Strain the liquid into another small saucepan and discard the solids. Add sugar and lemon juice to the tea. Simmer on medium heat until reduced to a syrup consistency, about 8 minutes. Allow to cool and chill in the refrigerator until ready to use.

TO SERVE  Onto each of six plates, place a tuile in the centre. Add ¼ cup of ice cream, pressing down gently to flatten the surface. Place another tuile on top of the ice cream. Sprinkle a sixth of the raspberries on top of the tuile and finish with a drizzle of syrup overtop.

SUGGESTED WINE  The intense fresh fruit of a Muscat de Beaume de Venise complements the raspberry and lemon flavours in this dessert perfectly. Moscato d'Asti's slightly spritzy, lively, grapey, orange-blossom nature makes a nimble pairing as well.

# à la pêche

1 cup water

2 Tbsp jasmine green tea leaves

¾ cup sugar

À LA PÊCHE COCKTAIL

½ slice fresh jalapeño,
about ¹⁄₁₆ inch thick

½ ripe organic peach,
peeled and pitted

1 oz Juniper Green
organic or other gin

1 oz Giffard Crème de Pêche
or other peach liqueur

½ oz freshly squeezed lime juice

¾ oz jasmine green tea syrup

1 slice cucumber, approximately
dime-thick, for garnish

This drink makes use of a favourite British Columbian orchard fruit and offers the contrast of peachy sweetness with a hint of spice from the jalapeño lifted with the floral notes of jasmine and a fresh note from the cucumber. If you let this cocktail sit, the heat from the jalapeño will grow, and the flavour of the cucumber will also rise in prominence.

JASMINE GREEN TEA SYRUP  Bring water to boil in a kettle. Place tea leaves in a French press and add boiling water. Allow to steep for 5 to 6 minutes and press. Pour into a small saucepan and add sugar. Bring to a simmer and cook until the sugar is fully dissolved. Allow to cool, then store in a jar or container with a secure lid. The resulting jasmine green tea syrup will last approximately one week before natural fermentation will occur. If you would like the syrup to last longer, add 3 to 4 oz of vodka to the syrup to prevent fermentation.

À LA PÊCHE COCKTAIL  Place jalapeño into a mixing glass and smash with a muddling stick. Add peach and continue muddling until roughly mashed. Add gin, peach liqueur, lime juice and jasmine green tea syrup. Fill the mixing glass with ice and shake vigorously until the shaker is very cold to the touch. If necessary, adjust the balance of sweetness and acidity to taste with additional green tea syrup and lime juice. Using a cocktail strainer, strain into a chilled martini glass and float the cucumber on the surface for garnish. The fine pulp that passes through the cocktail strainer adds a nice textural element to the drink.

fall

# seasons
# of service

To Brian Hopkins, the point of West and its facilities is to serve the guest. Erin Evans, one of the head hostesses, says, "We make people feel welcome, to anticipate what the guest wants. It can be intimidating coming into a fine-dining room, but we try to make everyone feel at ease immediately. Perhaps most importantly, I want to be a welcoming presence at the front door." The first few moments are vital, and Erin says, "A restaurant has to be a place the client can connect with. The room should be beautiful, the food must be great, but the personal experience has to be wonderful as well."

After guests encounter Erin and Brian, they next see award-winning mixologist David Wolowidnyk behind the bar. David is organized and disciplined, and he runs a very tight ship in terms of stocking, inventory control and, above all, quality control. And as the face at the bar, he is the very first line of actual service for the West guest. "I feel it is important to greet each person, even if they are obviously not stopping at the bar. I think of the bar as a vital part of the evening, even for someone only walking by it twice and checking it out from their table from time to time."

People do sit down in front of him and say, "Make me something great." He will, by asking how their day has been, determining what kind of mood they are in. "I always ask if there is a core spirit they want, and if they want it savoury, fruity, a bit sweet—that sort of thing. And then I build around the basic spirit and try to come up with a drink that is just right for the guest, this evening."

Brian Hopkins ensures his people are sensitive to the nuances of each guest and each table, including how much information guests may want about the ingredients, the methodology applied to a certain dish, wine matches and even geography. "People sometimes really want to be educated, but even so, there have to be sensible boundaries, and our team has to be alive to that, since it is different every time out," says Brian. Some people will be fascinated to know the butter on each table comes from a specific little herd of special cows, which eat only certain grains and vegetation, yielding milk that is then hand churned. But while this matters greatly to some guests, others will simply taste the difference; still others may not be interested. In each instance there must be an assessment, a decision, after which an action or non-action is played out at each table. Stephanie Noel, past sous chef, explains her approach while she was at West: "If a client has never tried something that is a bit unusual, I like to give them something that will show them how good that can be, something like octopus, or sweetbreads. If you don't like mushrooms, we can do five dishes with mushrooms, and you will love it." As Jack Evrensel explains, "This is 'degree of difficulty' dining. So, just like in Olympic diving, if you don't try to do the more difficult things, you can't expect to achieve the higher marks. We accept that concept. We welcome it, in fact." But as Brian says, "People can be much less forgiving of us, even than other fine-dining establishments. We must hit the exact right notes every time."

Every day at 5 PM Brian will convene a pre-service meeting and lay out how busy he anticipates the restaurant will be, whether he expects any special-occasion guests and what particular variables are going to be in play during that night's service. One of the chefs will briefly explain any specials for that evening, what the tasting menus are about and what might warrant a little extra attention when servers introduce and explain the dishes at the table. The staff will discuss wine pairings, as well as anything that struck a big chord during a test run and what will tend to work best with the evening's dishes. The atmosphere is relaxed, informative, convivial, but the overwhelming sense is one of anticipation, of understanding and meeting guests' needs.

This pre-service meeting is for the front-of-house staff. The kitchen staff has already had their own briefing, and many of them have been on premises for many hours already, cutting, chopping, peeling, braising and doing all manner of prep work. They will already know that the pine mushrooms and squab arrived that very morning, that the red onions are superb, that the last of the heirloom tomatoes were gone by nine last evening, that the two new dishes available to diners tonight are worthy of an extra emphasis by servers, just to ensure they are not overlooked.

The experience at West never happens by accident, something Brian Hopkins readily acknowledges, but, as he says, "Sensitivity to the guest is something the most thorough procedural manual can never teach. It takes a certain intuition to really do this work well." Brian is always seeking ways to improve West, both in the short and long term, and he begins by building a solid foundation of passionate and knowledgeable staff. "I actually prefer hiring younger staff, simply because they are willing and able to learn," he explains. Corey Bauldry concurs: "The average age in the kitchen is twenty-four years or so. It is very hard work, sixteen-hour days sometimes, but [staff members] are learning skills and pursuing their passion."

He adds, "Brian is an embodiment of West; he never hires the same type of people. They are all different, and all bring a different energy to the room. It keeps us all fresh, and we never get stale or simply go through the motions. Never."

Says Brian Hopkins, "I try to teach my staff that each person, each table, is different. Let the table set the mood, and we take it from there."

# seared scallops with apricot purée and candied walnuts

3½ oz dried apricots

1 Tbsp extra-virgin olive oil

4 large scallops

1 lemon, halved

3 oz candied walnuts (page 235)

4 oz Dijon mustard greens, for garnish

*Serves 4*

Dijon mustard greens may be available at a specialty food store but if they aren't available, any small and intensely flavoured greens such as watercress will also work.

PLACE apricots in a small pot and cover with water. Simmer for approximately 2 hours until the apricots are completely soft. Remove apricots from the water and purée in a high-speed blender.

Heat olive oil in a small sauté pan on high heat. Add scallops and sear 1 to 2 minutes per side until golden brown. Squeeze lemon juice over top.

TO SERVE In the middle of each of four plates, smear a quarter of the apricot purée. Place a scallop to the side of the purée and sprinkle a quarter of the walnuts around the plate. Finish with a quarter of the mustard greens.

SUGGESTED WINE This dish would pair well with unoaked light whites with a bit of sweetness, like a German riesling from the Mosel or an off-dry chenin blanc.

# seared scallops with crisp berkshire
# pork belly and pear–ginger purée

PORK BELLY AND SCALLOPS

1¼ cups light soy sauce

1¼ cups mirin

⅔ cup rice wine vinegar

¼ oz bonito flakes (about 1 Tbsp)

1-lb piece of pork belly

4 tsp olive oil

12 medium scallops,
1½ lbs total

PEAR–GINGER PURÉE

2 tsp olive oil

2 tsp unsalted butter

2 pears, quartered and cored

¼ oz fresh ginger,
grated (about 2 tsp)

Juice of ½ lemon

1 tsp sugar

2 Tbsp water

*Serves 4*

Berkshire pork, also sold as kurobuta pork, is a three-hundred-year-old breed of pork originating in the royal swine hold of the House of Windsor. This recipe pairs this pork with preserved lemon, available in specialty food stores, and preserved ginger. Whole ginger preserved in syrup—not to be confused with Japanese pickled ginger—is available in Asian supermarkets.

PORK BELLY AND SCALLOPS  In a heatproof marinating dish, combine soy sauce, mirin, rice wine vinegar and bonito flakes. Score the skin of the pork belly in a criss-cross pattern and place the pork in the soy sauce mixture. Cover and marinate in the refrigerator for 24 hours.

Preheat the oven to 300°F.

Heat the marinating dish on medium heat until the marinade is gently boiling. Cover the dish, then place it in the oven until the pork is tender, about 2 hours. Remove the pork from the marinade and place it skin-side down on a flat tray. Top with another tray and a weight of at least 4½ lbs, and leave it to set in the refrigerator overnight. Reserve the marinade.

Soak four wooden or bamboo skewers in water for at least 30 minutes.

Remove the skin from the pork belly and trim away the fat. Cut the pork into two equal pieces, then divide each half into six to yield twelve pieces of pork. Slide three pieces onto each skewer.

Preheat the oven to 350°F.

Heat a medium non-stick, ovenproof sauté pan on high heat. Add skewers of pork, fat-side down, and roast for 2 minutes. Add 3 Tbsp of marinade, then place the pan in the oven for 4 to 5 minutes. Remove from heat and baste the skewers with the drippings in the pan.

Heat olive oil in a small non-stick sauté pan. Add scallops, then roast in the oven for 2 to 3 minutes.

*Recipe continued overleaf...*

# noisettes of veal sweetbreads
## with mushroom duxelle

1 lb veal sweetbread hearts

4 carrots, peeled

2 Tbsp olive oil

1 clove garlic, chopped

1 onion, finely diced

9 oz button mushrooms, finely chopped

10 sprigs thyme, leaves picked off and stem discarded

⅓ cup Madeira

⅔ cup whipping cream

8 tsp cold unsalted butter

3 pods cardamom

1 cup chicken stock (page 231)

¼ cup freshly squeezed orange juice

½ lemon

Deep-fried parsley for garnish (page 237)

*Serves 4*

Veal sweetbreads, when roasted, deliver a crunchy exterior and a creamy smooth but firm interior. If possible, ask your butcher for veal sweetbread hearts, as these are the best, but you can use the entire veal sweetbread or lamb sweetbreads as well.

SOAK sweetbreads for 2 hours in cold water. Extract them from the water, then place them in a large pot of salted water and bring to a boil. Remove from the water and chill in the refrigerator for 30 minutes or until cold, then peel off the fine membrane. Break into twelve equal pieces.

Cut the carrots into sticks 2 inches long and ¼ inch square; set aside the carrot trimmings. Bring a small pot of water to a boil. Add carrot sticks and blanch for 2 minutes, then drain and plunge them into an ice bath to refresh.

In a small sauté pan, heat 2 tsp of the olive oil on medium heat. Add the garlic and half of the onion, and sweat for 2 minutes. Add mushrooms and thyme, and cook until all excess moisture has evaporated, about 2 minutes. Deglaze with Madeira and continue to cook for 4 to 5 minutes, until almost all of the liquid has evaporated. Pour in cream and heat again until most of the liquid has evaporated, about 5 minutes. Season this mushroom duxelle with salt and pepper.

Finely cut the reserved carrot trimmings. In a small sauté pan, heat 2 tsp of the olive oil and 4 tsp of the butter on medium heat. Add the remaining half of the onion and sweat for 2 to 3 minutes. Add carrot trimmings and

cardamom, then cover with chicken stock and cook for 12 to 15 minutes until carrot is soft. Purée this mixture in a blender, then strain the liquid through a fine sieve into a small saucepan. Add orange juice. Heat this liquid on medium heat until the sauce is reduced to the consistency of cream, about 5 minutes. Whisk in 2 tsp of cold butter. Season this sauce with salt, pepper and a squeeze of lemon juice.

Heat the remaining 2 tsp of olive oil in a heavy-bottomed sauté pan on high heat. Season sweetbreads with salt and pepper, then add them to the pan. Sear for 1 to 2 minutes, then add the remaining 2 tsp of butter and heat it until it foams. Continue cooking sweetbreads until golden. Season with salt and pepper and drain on paper towels.

TO SERVE  On each of four plates, spoon a quarter of the mushroom duxelle. Drag a spoon through the duxelle to create a small channel. Arrange carrots in a pile at one end of the channel and place three pieces of sweetbread on top. Spoon the sauce into the channel and around the plate. Garnish with fried parsley.

SUGGESTED WINE  This dish calls for your finest aged Burgundy in the cellar to pair with the soft, delicate flavour of sweetbreads. The slight woodsy notes of the mushrooms and earthy Burgundy go hand and hand.

noisettes of veal sweetbreads

with mushroom duxelle

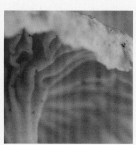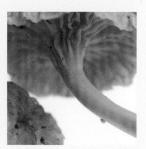

**ASK ANY MUSHROOM** hunter-gatherer to take you along on his or her next forage and you will encounter either a blank stare or a dismissive wave of the hand. A mushroom hunter's secrets are destined to remain so. Foraging is a skill that is developed over time, with a good amount of instinct thrown in and a keen knowledge of the effects of weather, forest conditions, seasonal fires and a variety of other factors.

Chanterelle mushrooms, *Cantherellis cibarius*, are relatively difficult to find, requiring on-your-knees, delicate hands-only harvesting. They are mycorrhizal fungi, relying on a symbiotic relationship with plants, most notably the Douglas-fir and Sitka spruce of the Pacific Northwest. This delicate interdependence is what makes them extremely difficult to cultivate, thus ensuring they are highly prized. Foraging is an intense, multi-million-dollar industry in British Columbia, and in peak season, people arrive from all over North America to set up tent and make their way through the equivalent of a culinary gold rush. Although purists may prefer these mushrooms slow-cooked over an open fire, chefs around the world prize them for their rich flavour and adaptability to a wide range of treatments. Mikuni Wild Harvest is a company that sources all kinds of foraged foods, such as fiddleheads and mushrooms, and is dedicated to buying freshly picked mushrooms from a reliable group of foragers. A select portion of these come to West, where the chefs' imaginations ramp immediately into high gear.

# chanterelle mushrooms

# spatchcock-roasted quail and crispy quail eggs with baby chanterelles and arugula

4 large quails, backbone removed

5 Tbsp olive oil

1 clove garlic, sliced

1 tsp fresh thyme leaves

1 sprig rosemary, leaves
picked off and coarsely chopped

10 black peppercorns, crushed

¼ cup white wine vinegar

4 cups water

8 quail eggs, peeled

1 tsp white truffle oil

2 Tbsp flour

1 hen's egg, lightly beaten

1 cup panko bread crumbs

¼ oz chives, chopped (about 1 Tbsp)

*Serves 4*

Spatchcock is a traditional cooking method for roasting and broiling game birds over a grill or spit and involves slicing out the backbone of the bird—something you can ask your butcher to do—and flattening it out prior to cooking. This recipe calls for panko, light and crispy bread crumbs from Japan that you can find at most Asian supermarkets, and truffle oil, available at specialty food stores.

SOAK eight large bamboo skewers in water for about 8 hours or overnight.

Run a skewer through the left leg and right breast of each quail. Then run a skewer through the right leg and left breast so that the skewers cross. In a small bowl, combine 3 Tbsp of the olive oil, garlic, thyme, rosemary and peppercorns. Spread this marinade over the quails and allow to marinate for at least 6 hours, preferably overnight.

Combine white wine vinegar and water in a medium pot and bring the mixture to a boil. Crack a quail egg into the water and poach for 30 seconds. Carefully remove the egg with a slotted spoon and place it into an ice bath. Repeat with the remaining quail eggs until all of them have been poached. Transfer the eggs from the ice bath into a small bowl. Add truffle oil and allow to marinate for 8 to 12 hours or overnight.

Place flour in a shallow dish and the hen's egg in another shallow dish. Mix bread crumbs and chives in a third shallow dish. Carefully dip each poached quail egg first into the flour to dredge, then into the beaten egg, then in the bread crumbs to coat. Store in an airtight container, leaving space between the eggs, until ready to fry.

4½ oz double-smoked bacon,
½ inch thick, frozen
and cut into ¾-inch pieces

24 baby chanterelles

1 shallot, finely diced

5 tsp sherry vinegar

5 tsp chicken stock (page 231)

2 tsp cold unsalted butter

¼ oz flat-leaf parsley,
chopped (about 2 tsp)

4 cups vegetable oil, for deep frying

7 oz arugula

In a small sauté pan, heat 1 Tbsp of the olive oil on medium heat. Add bacon and sauté for 5 minutes until golden brown, then add chanterelles and shallot and sauté for another 5 minutes. Deglaze the pan with sherry vinegar, then add chicken stock and cook until liquid is reduced to a syrup, about 5 minutes. Add butter and whisk to emulsify. Add parsley and season with salt and pepper. Keep warm.

Preheat the oven to 400°F.

In a large ovenproof sauté pan, heat the remaining 1 Tbsp of olive oil on high heat. Add quails and sear about 2 minutes, turning once, until both sides are golden brown. Roast in the oven for 5 minutes, then remove from heat and allow to rest for 10 minutes.

Heat vegetable oil in a deep fryer or a deep pot to 350°F. Add quail eggs and fry for 30 seconds until golden brown. Remove from the oil and season with salt.

TO SERVE Remove the skewers from the quails and place each bird in the middle of a plate. Spoon a quarter of the mushrooms and sprinkle a quarter of the arugula leaves overtop. Lay a fried quail egg on top of the arugula.

SUGGESTED WINE Bourgueil or Chinon, both made from the cabernet franc grape, are good for the roasted quail. They add spicy, woodsy herbal notes of their own for the chanterelles and arugula.

# squab breasts with a warm
## parfait of pears and pine mushrooms

4 pears, peeled,
quartered and cored

½ cup cold unsalted butter

6-8 small pine mushrooms, cleaned

5 tsp port

5 tsp Madeira

5 tsp brandy

1 sprig thyme

2 shallots, one sliced
and one finely diced

4 squabs, 1 lb each

1 clove garlic, finely diced

5½ oz fresh chicken livers

1 egg

2 oz golden raisins,
soaked in water to rehydrate

1 oz walnuts, chopped

2 tsp olive oil

⅓ cup roasting jus (page 232)

3½ oz baby spinach

*Serves 4*

Squab is a rich but lean bird, a young pigeon. It should be available through a specialty butcher.

SLICE two of the pears thinly lengthwise. Heat 2 tsp of the butter in a non-stick pan on high heat. Add pear slices and sauté until caramelized, about 1 minute per side.

Line four 2½-inch ramekins with plastic wrap, then line the bottom and the side of each ramekin with the pear slices.

Cut the remaining two pears into ¼-inch dice. Heat 2 tsp of the butter in a small non-stick sauté pan on high heat. Add pear dice and sauté until caramelized, about 3 minutes.

Cut the stems off the pine mushrooms to within ½ inch of the cap and dice the stems. In a small sauté pan, heat 2 tsp of the butter on high heat. Add diced stems and sauté for about 1 minute.

In a small saucepan, heat port, Madeira, brandy, thyme and the sliced shallot on medium heat until reduced to a syrup, about 5 minutes.

Remove the livers and hearts from the squab and clean them. Cut the squab livers and hearts into ¼-inch dice. In a small sauté pan, heat 1 tsp of the butter on medium heat. Add the diced shallot and garlic and sweat for 3 to 4 minutes until soft. Add the squab livers and hearts and cook for 1 minute.

Preheat the oven to 250°F and melt ¼ cup of the butter in the microwave. In a food processor, blend together 3½ oz of the chicken livers and the port reduction, then add the melted butter and egg. Season the mixture with salt and pepper, then pass it through a fine sieve. Fold in the shallot and squab liver mixture, raisins, walnuts, diced pear and diced mushroom stems.

Transfer this parfait mixture to an earthenware dish and cover it with aluminum foil. Place the earthenware dish in a larger baking dish. Pour boiling

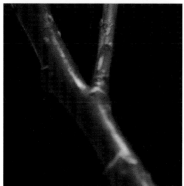

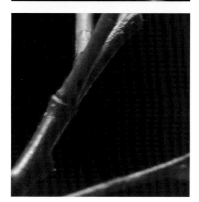

water into the baking dish to make a bain marie. Place in the oven and cook for 25 to 30 minutes.

Remove from the oven and allow to cool. Spoon the parfait into the lined moulds and bake them in the oven for 8 to 10 minutes.

Raise the oven temperature to 350°F.

In a large sauté pan, heat olive oil on high heat. Add squabs and sear for 2 minutes per side. Transfer to the oven and roast for 7 to 8 minutes. Remove the legs and return them to the oven for another 3 or 4 minutes while the squab crowns rest at room temperature.

Bring roasting jus to boil, add the remaining 2 oz of chicken livers, simmer for 30 seconds, then purée in a blender. Pass through a fine sieve, then whisk in 1 tsp of cold butter. Season to taste with salt and pepper.

Quarter the pine mushroom caps. In a small sauté pan, heat 2 tsp of the butter on low heat. Add mushroom caps and cook for 2 minutes. Season with salt and pepper.

In a small sauté pan, heat the remaining 2 tsp of butter on medium heat. Add spinach and sauté until just wilted, about 30 seconds.

TO SERVE Unmould each parfait and place it on one side of a plate. On the opposite side, heap a quarter of the spinach. Carve the breasts off the squab and lay them on top of the spinach. Lean squab legs on either side of the breasts. Sprinkle a quarter of the mushroom caps around each plate, then spoon a quarter of the port sauce overtop.

SUGGESTED WINE The concentrated silky smooth pinot noirs of the Willamette Valley in Oregon make a grand pairing with this dish.

SHOULD YOU VISIT the Champagne region of France in late autumn you will likely discover that in virtually every fine-dining establishment in the region, the seasonal house specialty is *pigeonneau*. These delicate, moist, quite dark-meated birds, dressed for market before ever taking flight, are in fact young pigeons raised specifically for an appearance at the dinner table. They are known in North America as squab.

Squab meat retains its moisture well through all manner of cooking methods, so no wonder chefs enjoy working with it. The bird has been considered a royal delicacy for many centuries, in Asia and in the Arabic world. Even now, both in Europe and on this continent, squab seems more likely to appear in a fine-dining context than anywhere else. Still, producers in B.C. cannot meet demand. They dress over sixty thousand birds for market each year, but that number is supplemented by more than a hundred thousand imported birds, frozen and shipped from California, itself a hotbed of squab production. Thiessen Farms, in British Columbia's Fraser Valley, takes particular care, using special feeds and an uncrowded, clean environment for their birds. This attention ensures a pristine, fresh bird for the chefs, and the guests, at West.

squab

squab with lobster, kabocha
squash and rosemary beignets

# squab and lobster with kabocha squash
# and rosemary beignets

BEIGNETS

1 Kabocha squash, 8 oz

1 clove garlic, sliced

1 sprig thyme, leaves picked
off and stems discarded

4 tsp olive oil

1 sprig rosemary, leaves stripped
off and very finely chopped

1 oz pine nuts, toasted

Lobster knuckle meat
from squab and lobster

7 oz pasta dough (page 237)

1 egg

1 egg yolk

4 cups vegetable oil for deep frying

*Serves 4*

Kabocha squash is a Japanese pumpkin. It is sweeter, drier and less fibrous than other squash. If you cannot find Kabocha squash, butternut squash would make an ideal substitute. After you cook the lobster, set aside the knuckle meat to make the beignets.

BEIGNETS  Preheat the oven to 275°F. Cut squash in quarters and remove seeds. Place the squash onto a large sheet of aluminum foil and sprinkle with garlic, thyme, salt and pepper. Drizzle the squash with olive oil. Fold up the ends of the foil to form a parcel and place it in the oven for 1½ to 2 hours. When squash is soft, scoop out all the flesh and pass it through a fine sieve. Set aside.

SQUAB AND LOBSTER  Bring court bouillon to a boil, add lobsters and remove from heat immediately. Allow to cool for 1 hour, uncovered.

Remove wing tips and neck from squab and set these trimmings aside. Cut each squab down both sides of the breastbone and straight through the carcass to form two halves. Coarsely chop the central bones left behind.

In a large, heavy-bottomed pot, heat 2 tsp of the olive oil and 2 tsp of the butter on high heat. Add squab trimmings, including the chopped bones, and roast on the stove until golden brown, about 10 minutes, stirring frequently. Add 1 sprig of thyme and half of each of the carrot, onion, celery and garlic. Continue to roast for another 6 to 8 minutes. Cover with 2 cups of cold water, bring to a boil and simmer gently for 45 minutes.

Remove the lobsters from the bouillon. Crack the shells and remove the meat from the tails, claws and knuckles, reserving the shells. Wash the heads thoroughly to remove all entrails. Set the lobster meat aside in the refrigerator.

In a large, heavy-bottomed pot, heat 2 tsp of the olive oil and 2 tsp of the butter on high heat. Add lobster shells and roast on the stove for about

8 cups court bouillon (page 229)

2 lobsters, 1 lb each

2 squabs, 1 lb each

2 Tbsp olive oil

2½ Tbsp unsalted butter

2 sprigs thyme

1 carrot, chopped

1 onion, chopped

3 ribs celery, chopped

2 cloves garlic, chopped

4 cups cold water

1 tsp tomato paste

4 tsp brandy

5½ oz baby spinach

10 minutes, stirring frequently. Add the remaining sprig of thyme and the remaining half of the carrot, celery, onion and garlic, and continue to roast for another 6 to 8 minutes. Add tomato paste and brandy, and cook for a further 2 minutes. Cover with the remaining 2 cups of cold water, bring to a boil and then simmer gently for 45 minutes.

Strain both stocks through cheesecloth and combine them in a large saucepan. Heat on medium heat and allow to reduce to the consistency of cream, about 20 minutes. Keep this sauce warm on low heat.

Preheat the oven to 400°F. In a large, ovenproof sauté pan on high heat, combine 2 tsp of the olive oil and 2 tsp of the butter. Season squab with salt and pepper and add to the pan, skin-side down. Brown for 2 minutes, then turn the squab over and place the pan in the oven for 3 to 4 minutes. Remove the pan from the oven and separate the squab legs from the breasts. Return the legs to the pan and the pan to the oven for a further 4 minutes while the breasts rest at room temperature.

Cut lobster tail in half lengthwise. Place all of the lobster meat in the sauce and warm on low heat for 6 to 8 minutes until the lobster is heated through. Remove the lobster meat and whisk the remaining 4 tsp of cold butter into the sauce to finish. Chop the lobster knuckle meat for the beignets.

TO SERVE Place squash in a large bowl. Fold in rosemary, pine nuts and chopped lobster knuckle meat.

Roll out pasta into two sheets, each 12 inches × 6 inches and the thickness of a dime. Along the centre line of one pasta sheet, spoon eight portions of the squash mixture about 1½ inches apart.

*Recipe continued overleaf. . .*

Lightly beat together egg, egg yolk and a pinch of salt to make an egg wash. Brush the edges of the pasta and between the fillings with egg wash. Lay the second sheet on top and press along the edges and between the fillings to seal. Cut the pasta between the fillings to yield eight ravioli.

Heat oil in a deep fryer to 400°F. Add ravioli and fry for 3 minutes. Remove from the oil and allow them to drain on paper towels.

In a small sauté pan, heat 2 tsp of olive oil on high heat. Add spinach and sauté for 30 to 45 seconds until just wilted.

Heap a quarter of the spinach just off the centre of each of four plates. Carve a squab breast from the bone and cut it in half on a bias. Place the breast on the spinach and lean a squab leg against it. Opposite the squab, place half a lobster tail and top with a claw. Drizzle 4 tsp of sauce overtop and top with two squash beignets.

SUGGESTED WINE This outstanding dish calls for a grand wine and is an opportunity to pull out that powerful and silky smooth aged grand cru red burgundy from the cellar. Vineyards from the Côte de Nuits that would make a memorable pairing would be Chambertin, Le Musigny, Echézeaux or Clos de la Roche.

# aromatic pine mushroom and duck broth with
# smoked scallops and black truffle oil

2 Tbsp vegetable oil

2 lbs duck bones, chopped
into 2-inch pieces

2 pieces calf's foot, about 8 oz each

1 onion, quartered

1 carrot, split lengthwise

1 rib celery

1 leek

4 cloves garlic

1 sprig thyme

1 bay leaf

½ Tbsp coriander seeds, toasted

½ Tbsp cumin seeds, toasted

2 pods star anise

1 cup Madeira

½ cup light soy sauce

10 cups water

2 pine mushrooms, cut into
dime-thick slices on a mandolin

SMOKED SCALLOPS

4 large, fresh scallops, cut in half

1 Tbsp coarse salt

1 duck confit leg,
shredded (page 238)

1/4 oz chives, chopped (about 1 Tbsp)

4 tsp black truffle oil

*Serves 4*

This dish calls for a calf's foot: your butcher should be able to bring one in if you ask for it in advance. To smoke the scallops, you will need one piece of charcoal and a handful of wood chips. Soak the chips in water for about 5 minutes before using. You will also need a stainless-steel pot with a lid and a wire insert that will hold the scallops above the smouldering wood chips.

DUCK BROTH  Preheat the oven to 325°F. Heat vegetable oil in a roasting pan on high heat. Add duck bones, then place the pan in the oven for about 30 minutes until the bones are golden brown, stirring occasionally. Strain off the fat and place bones into a stock pot. Add calf's foot, onions, carrots, celery, leek, garlic, thyme, bay leaf, coriander seeds, cumin seeds, star anise, Madeira, soy sauce and water. Cover and bring to a slow simmer. Cook for 2½ hours. The liquid must barely simmer so that it stays clear. Pass the broth through a cheesecloth into another pot.

SMOKED SCALLOPS  Coat the scallops with coarse salt and allow them to sit for 1 hour. Rinse off the salt and pat the scallops dry with a kitchen towel.

Preheat the oven to 400°F. Heat the charcoal in the oven for 15 minutes, then remove it from the oven and ignite it with a kitchen torch. Allow it to burn for 3 minutes. Place the charcoal in a solid stainless-steel pot. Sprinkle wood chips on and around the charcoal. Place the scallops on a wire rack 4 inches above the charcoal and cover the pot. Allow the scallops to smoke for 20 minutes.

TO SERVE  Place the pine mushrooms into the broth and allow them to infuse for 3 minutes. In each of four bowls, place a quarter of the duck confit, smoked scallops and chives. Ladle a quarter of the broth overtop, and finish each serving with 1 tsp of black truffle oil.

SUGGESTED WINE  A rich, dry California traditional-method rosé sparkling wine would work very well with the smoky, earthy flavours of this dish.

# pork loin, belly and ravioli with apple-cinnamon purée and eggplant caviar

1 lb pork belly

1½ cups soy sauce

1 cup mirin

½ cup rice wine vinegar

3 slices fresh ginger

1 Tbsp bonito flakes

1½ lbs bone-in pork loin, cleaned

5 carrots, coarsely chopped

5 ribs celery, coarsely chopped

3 onions, peeled
and coarsely chopped

3 sprigs thyme

6 bay leaves

¾ cup + 2 Tbsp olive oil

1 lb pork cheeks

8 oz pork tongue

Pinch of Chinese five-spice powder

1 cup white wine

6 cups chicken stock (page 231)

2 cups brown veal and chicken jus
(page 232)

3 small dill pickles, chopped

1 lb pasta dough (page 237)

3 Tbsp butter

3 cups vegetable oil for deep-frying

1 cup flour for dredging

4 baby bok choy

*Serves 4*

SEARED PORK AND RAVIOLI  Place the pork belly in a shallow bowl. In a small bowl, mix together soy sauce, mirin, rice wine vinegar, ginger and bonito flakes. Pour this mixture over the pork belly and marinate for 24 hours.

Preheat the oven to 350°F.

Cut the pork loin into four thick chops and refrigerate until needed. Cut the pork bones into 2-inch pieces and place them in a roasting pan. Roast the bones in the oven until golden brown, about 30 minutes.

Combine carrots, celery, onions, thyme and bay leaves in a large bowl.

Heat 2 Tbsp of olive oil in a large, heavy-bottomed pot on medium-high heat. Add one-third of the vegetables and herbs and roast until golden brown, about 10 minutes.

In a medium sauté pan, heat another 2 Tbsp of olive oil. Add pork cheeks and sear for 3 minutes on both sides on medium heat. Add the cheeks to the roasted vegetables. Also add pork tongue, five-spice powder and wine and cook on medium heat until wine has reduced by half, about 15 minutes. Cover with chicken stock and veal and chicken jus. Cover the mixture with a cartouche—a round of parchment paper cut to the diameter of the pot with a hole in the centre to allow steam to escape—and braise in the oven for 2 hours, or until tender. Drain and set aside in the refrigerator.

In a large, heavy-bottomed pot, heat 2 Tbsp of olive oil on medium-high heat. Add one-third of the unroasted vegetables and herbs and roast until golden brown, about 10 minutes. Add the roasted bones. Cover with the braising liquid, then simmer on medium-low heat for 1½ hours. Strain the liquid through a sieve into a large saucepan and continue to cook on medium heat until it has reduced by three-quarters, or until the sauce sticks to the back of a spoon, about 5 minutes. Strain this pork jus again through a fine sieve and cheesecloth and set aside.

*Recipe continued overleaf. . .*

BABY FENNEL GARNISH

¼ cup extra-virgin olive oil

1 shallot, sliced

Peels from 2 oranges

1 sprig thyme

1 bay leaf

8 bulbs baby fennel

¾ cup chicken stock (page 231)

DEEP-FRIED CELERY LEAVES

1 cup vegetable oil

12 celery leaves—use the tender, light green leaves from the heart of the stalk

and sear until light brown, about 6 minutes. Place in the oven and roast for 5 minutes. Remove from the oven and allow to rest for 6 minutes.

Meanwhile, slice fingerling potatoes in half lengthwise. In a small sauté pan, heat butter on medium heat and add potatoes. Sauté for about 10 minutes until brown, turning potatoes every 2 minutes or so, and keep warm.

BABY FENNEL GARNISH Heat olive oil in a medium sauté pan on medium heat. Add shallot, orange peel, thyme and bay leaf and sauté until shallot is soft, about 5 minutes. Add baby fennel and season with salt and pepper. Cover with chicken stock and bring to a simmer for about 20 minutes, or until fennel is fully cooked. Remove fennel with a slotted spoon and set aside. Reduce the braising liquid by half, about 8 minutes.

DEEP-FRIED CELERY LEAVES Heat oil in a deep fryer or a medium pot to 350°F. Plunge celery leaves into the oil and fry for 5 seconds. Remove them from the oil, lightly sprinkle them with salt and allow them to drain on paper towels.

TO SERVE Return the fennel to its sauce and warm on low heat. Slice each rabbit saddle into six slices.

On each of four plates, place two pieces of fennel in the middle along with half a potato and three slices of rabbit. Finish with a quarter of the rabbit sauce and garnish with the celery leaves.

SUGGESTED WINE Medium-bodied Italian reds go very well with rabbit. A Chianti Riserva's dried cherry fruit balances the saltiness of the prosciutto here, and the fennel in the dish brings out a concordant note in the wine. A Barbera d'Alba from a good producer would make a fine substitute.

# fillet of ling cod with roasted fennel and ragout of calamari

## CALAMARI RAGOUT

2 squid, 9 oz each, cleaned
and tentacles removed

4 tsp olive oil

¼ onion, finely chopped

1 clove garlic, finely chopped

4 tsp thyme leaves

½ cup red wine

⅔ cup fish stock (page 229)

¼ cup roasting jus (page 232)

4 tsp whipping cream

4 tsp unsalted butter

1 oz parsley, chopped (about 3 Tbsp)

## ROASTED FENNEL

2 bulbs fennel, cut into
20 batons of 2 inches × ¼ inch,
with trimmings reserved

5 Tbsp unsalted butter

¼ cup chicken stock (page 231)

¼ cup whipping cream

## ROASTED LING COD FILLET

2 tsp olive oil

4 ling cod fillets, 4½ oz each

½ lemon

*Serves 4*

CALAMARI RAGOUT  Cut the squid tubes into rings ¼ inch wide and wash them. In a heavy-bottomed pan on medium heat, add olive oil. Add onion, garlic and thyme and sweat until onion is translucent but not browned, about 5 minutes.

Add squid rings and cook for a further 5 minutes. Add wine and fish stock, then simmer gently, stirring frequently, until almost all the liquid has evaporated, about 30 minutes. Add roasting jus and simmer for another 5 minutes. If the squid is not tender, add water in ¼-cup increments and continue to simmer until it is. Finish with cream, butter and parsley.

ROASTED FENNEL  Bring a medium pot of water to a boil. Add fennel batons and blanch for 2 minutes, then plunge them into an ice bath to refresh. Heat 2 Tbsp of the butter in a medium sauté pan on high heat until it foams. Add fennel batons and roast for 3 minutes. Season with salt and pepper.

Finely chop the fennel trimmings.

Heat 1 Tbsp of the butter in a medium sauté pan on medium heat. Add half of the fennel trimmings and sweat until soft, about 10 minutes. Add chicken stock, cook until liquid evaporates, about 5 minutes, then purée in a blender and pass through a fine sieve.

Place the rest of the fennel trimmings in a small saucepan and just cover with cold water. Bring to a boil, simmer for 5 minutes, then purée in a blender and strain through a cheesecloth, reserving the liquid only. Measure out 2 cups of this liquid and add cream and the remaining 2 Tbsp of the butter. *Recipe continued overleaf. . .*

ROASTED LING COD FILLET  Preheat the oven to 350°F. Heat a large oven-proof, non-stick pan on high heat. Add olive oil, followed by the ling cod, skin-side down. Transfer the pan to the oven and cook for 5 to 7 minutes. Remove from heat and season with salt, pepper and a squeeze of lemon juice.

TO SERVE  Vigorously whisk the fennel and cream mixture until it forms a foam. In the centre of each of four bowls, spoon 2 tsp of fennel purée. Top with 4 tsp of calamari ragout, then lay five fennel batons on top. Place a ling cod fillet in the bowl, then finish with the fennel foam.

SUGGESTED WINE  Although full-bodied whites like Russian River chardonnay or Northern Rhône Condrieu would enhance the flavours of this dish, this is a good opportunity to drink red wine with fish. Try a red with low, soft, velvety tannins like pinot noirs from Central Otago or Santa Barbara, which have a rich, creamy palate to match the sweet anise flavour of the fennel.

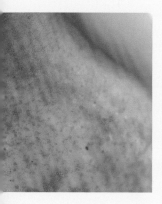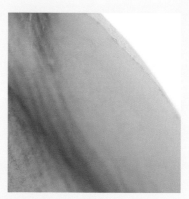

THE PEAR'S uncultivated history can be traced to the Tien Shan foothills in western China, but the three best-known pear varieties, D'Anjou, Bartlett and Bosc, were first cultivated in Europe. They were (unsuccessfully) planted by early settlers on the east coast of this continent and (successfully) a little later in Washington, Oregon, and the Okanagan and Similkameen valleys of British Columbia. Pears are picked by hand before they are fully ripened and are distinguishable from their close cousin the apple by their large number of lignified cells known as "grit."

British Columbia produces 37 million pounds of pears per year, give or take a bushel. China, by contrast, produces nearly 20 billion pounds. The French have a method of tying empty bottles to trees, containing the pear in its flowering stage within the bottle's interior. The fruit grows to maturity, and the entire thing, bottle and pear, is plucked from the tree, filled with grain spirit and aged. This is the short version of how the famous *eau de vie* is made. Not all bottles actually contain a pear, but it is worth seeking out one that does.

Pears taken fresh and uncooked are juicy and sweet, although the Bosc has a notably firmer, drier texture that makes it ideal for baking. Poaching, sautéing, baking—it all works well with pears, and their flavour can be the backbone of a myriad of interesting dishes.

# pears

# sherry-poached pears with a pear and raisin compote and maple-roasted walnuts

POACHED AND ROASTED PEARS

4 ripe Bartlett pears

1¼ cups oloroso sherry

⅓ cup sugar

Zest of ½ orange

¼ tsp ground black pepper

¼ cup raisins

2 Tbsp honey

Juice of ½ lemon

MAPLE-ROASTED WALNUTS

¾ cup walnuts

¼ cup maple syrup

CRISPY FILO

1 tsp honey

1 Tbsp unsalted butter, melted

2 sheets filo dough

*Serves 4*

POACHED AND ROASTED PEARS  Peel, core and slice off the bottom half of each pear. Dice the bottom halves and set aside. Place pear tops in a medium saucepan with sherry, sugar and orange zest and simmer until tender, about 1 hour. Allow to cool. Remove pear tops from the liquid and set aside. Heat ¾ cup of the liquid on medium heat until reduced to a syrup, about 15 minutes.

Preheat the oven to 350°F. In a small roasting pan, combine diced pears, black pepper, raisins, honey and lemon juice. Roast this mixture in the oven, stirring periodically, until pears are tender but not mushy, about 30 minutes. Remove from the oven and allow to cool.

MAPLE-ROASTED WALNUTS  Preheat the oven to 350°F. Spread nuts on a baking sheet and lightly toast them in the oven for 10 minutes. Shake off and discard the skin from the nuts. Drizzle nuts with syrup and toss to coat. Return to the oven and, stirring every 5 minutes, bake until all the maple syrup has crystallized, about 20 minutes.

CRISPY FILO  Preheat the oven to 325°F and line a baking sheet with parchment paper. Whisk together honey and butter and brush onto one sheet of filo dough. Place the other sheet on top and flatten with a rolling pin. Brush the top with the honey butter. Cut the dough into dime-thick strips and lay them out on the baking sheet. Bake about 10 minutes until golden brown.

TO SERVE  Roughly chop walnuts and toss with roasted pear mixture. Divide the pear and walnut mixture among four ring moulds the same diameter as the pear tops, pressing down gently with the back of a spoon. Carefully remove rings. Place the poached pear on top and drizzle sherry reduction over the pear. Sprinkle filo strips around the pear to look like a nest.

SUGGESTED WINE  Try a very good cream or Pedro Ximénez sherry.

# pink lady apple mascarpone confit with apple-rosemary ice cream and hazelnut praline

### APPLE CONFIT

4 Pink Lady apples,
peeled, cored and halved

¾ cup brown sugar

¾ cup mascarpone

⅓ cup lemon juice

### APPLE-ROSEMARY ICE CREAM

1 apple, peeled,
cored and roughly diced

¾ cup whipping cream

⅓ cup whole milk

1 sprig rosemary

6 egg yolks

½ cup brown sugar

### HAZELNUT PRALINE

¾ cup hazelnuts

¾ cup sugar

5 Tbsp water

¼ cup unsalted butter

*Serves 6*

APPLE CONFIT  Preheat the oven to 350°F. Line a 6-inch square cake pan with parchment paper. Cut each apple half into slices about ¹⁄₁₆ inch thick and lay the slices into the pan, slightly overlapping the slices to cover the bottom of the pan. Sprinkle about a quarter of the brown sugar, spoon a quarter of the mascarpone and drizzle a quarter of the lemon juice on the layer of apples.

Repeat layering of apples, sugar, mascarpone and lemon juice until all apples are used. The pan should have about four layers of apples.

Bake for 30 minutes. Press down on apples with a spatula to flatten the top surface. Bake another 40 minutes, or until a knife pierces the apples easily and most of the liquid has evaporated.

Allow to cool, then chill in the refrigerator for about 2 hours before cutting.

Flip the cake pan upside down onto a cutting board. With a sharp, serrated knife, trim off the edges and cut the apple confit into 2-inch squares.

APPLE-ROSEMARY ICE CREAM  In a medium saucepan, simmer apple, cream, milk and rosemary until apples are cooked and falling apart, about 20 minutes. Whisk together yolks and sugar in a medium heatproof mixing bowl until the mixture is a pale yellow. Slowly add the hot milk mixture, whisking vigorously to prevent eggs from curdling. Return custard to the saucepan and cook on high heat, stirring constantly, until the mixture coats the back of a spoon. Allow to cool and remove the rosemary.

Purée the apple mixture in a blender and strain it through a fine sieve. Pour the mixture into an ice cream machine and process according to the manufacturer's instructions.

HAZELNUT PRALINE Preheat the oven to 350°F. Spread hazelnuts onto a baking sheet and toast them in the oven until they are light brown on the inside, about 20 minutes, and rub off excess skin. In a food processor, grind nuts very fine until they resemble the texture of cornmeal.

In a small saucepan, bring sugar and water to a boil and cook until caramel in colour, about 10 minutes. Add hazelnuts and butter and mix well.

Preheat the oven to 325°F.

Lay out a piece of parchment paper on the counter. Pour praline mixture onto the parchment paper. Add another sheet of parchment on top and roll flat to about ¹⁄₁₆ inch thick. Pull off top sheet of parchment and slide the praline sheet onto a baking sheet. Place in the oven until the praline bubbles slightly, about 10 minutes.

Remove from the oven and lay a sheet of parchment on top. With a rolling pin, roll the praline as thin as you can, to about the thickness of a dime.

Allow to cool, then break into shards about 2 inches wide and keep them in an airtight container until needed.

TO SERVE On each of six plates, place a square of apple confit, then top with a ¼-cup scoop of ice cream. Garnish with shard of praline in the ice cream.

SUGGESTED WINE A five-puttonyos Tokaj's intense pit-fruit density attends to the apple, and its woodsy spice finish transforms the rosemary ice cream's single note into an orchestra of flavours. Canadian late-harvest vidal makes a good pairing as well. Its leafy intensity likes both the apple and the rosemary very well.

# raisin pecan crackers and melted camembert
# with grape compote and icewine sorbet

2 cups flour

¼ cup brown sugar

1 tsp salt

1 tsp baking soda

½ cup raisins

1 cup whole pecans, shelled

2 tsp molasses

¾ cup yogurt

¼ cup apple juice

1 tsp honey

1 wheel of Camembert, about 8 oz, halved, then cut into a total of 12 half-moon slices

CONCORD GRAPE COMPOTE

¼ cup fireweed honey

¼ vanilla bean, split and scraped, but pod reserved

1¼ cups Concord grapes, destemmed

*Serves 4*

RAISIN PECAN CRACKERS  In a large mixing bowl, combine flour, sugar, salt, baking soda, raisins, pecans, molasses, yogurt, apple juice and honey to form a very sticky dough. Pour onto a piece of parchment paper 12 inches square and form into a cylinder about 2½ inches in diameter. Roll the cylinder up in the parchment paper, twisting the ends closed.

Preheat the oven to 325°F.

Place parchment-wrapped dough in a loaf pan and bake 40 to 60 minutes, until the loaf springs back when pressed.

Remove from the oven and allow to cool.

Remove the parchment and cut the cylinder into very thin slices (about ¹⁄₁₆ inch thick) with a sharp serrated knife.

Lay slices out onto a baking sheet and return to the oven to dry until just crispy and not too brown, about 10 minutes. Store in an airtight container until ready to use.

CONCORD GRAPE COMPOTE  In a medium sauté pan, heat honey and vanilla bean (both seeds and pod) on medium heat until bubbles form, about 2 minutes. Toss the grapes in the honey and stir until they are heated through. Remove and discard the vanilla pod.

ICEWINE GRAPE SORBET  In a medium saucepan, combine grapes, water and vanilla bean (both seeds and pod) and cook on medium heat until the skins burst. Allow to cool, then remove and discard the vanilla pod. Purée the grape mixture in a blender and strain the liquid into a medium bowl through a fine sieve, discarding the solids. Add icewine. Chill in the refrigerator until cold, about 1 hour, then pour into an electric ice cream machine and process according to the manufacturer's instructions.

ICEWINE GRAPE SORBET

1¼ cups Concord
grapes, destemmed

⅓ cup water

¼ vanilla bean, split and
scraped, but pod reserved

¾ cup icewine

TO SERVE  Preheat the oven to 350°F. On each of four plates, lay out three crackers. Top each cracker with a piece of cheese and about a tablespoon of the grape compote. Stack the crackers on top of one another in the centre of the plate and place the plates in the oven for 5 minutes, or until the cheese has melted. Remove from the oven, top the crackers with a 2-Tbsp scoop of sorbet and serve.

SUGGESTED WINE  The wine you use to prepare the dish is usually the best pairing. Canadian icewine is always a treat and is prized around the world. B.C. icewine is often best drunk as a dessert in itself, but the freshness of the grape compote and the smooth, creamy camembert in this dessert offer a contrast that works well.

# four o'clock

VANILLA CITRUS FOAM

5 oz Navan vanilla cognac

5 oz freshly squeezed orange juice

4 oz freshly squeezed lemon juice

10 oz simple syrup (page 235)

2 tsp orange blossom water

6 gelatin leaves, softened
in a little cold water

FOUR O'CLOCK COCKTAIL

1 cube sugar

½ oz water

3-4 dashes Fee Brothers
whiskey barrel-aged bitters

1 oz Maker's Mark bourbon

1 oz Grand Marnier Louis Alexander

½ oz freshly squeezed lemon juice

Vanilla citrus foam, for garnish

Inspired by the old-fashioned whisky cocktail, this drink has been updated with a vanilla–orange blossom foam garnish that lends added flavour to the experience. It offers a slightly sweet yet tart candylike entrance through the foam, leading to a savoury bourbon experience with a touch of clove and cinnamon from the bitters, and a slight spiciness on the finish. As the drink warms up, the foam collapses into a liquid, adding another dimension to the cocktail. To make the foam, you will need a whipped cream dispenser.

VANILLA CITRUS FOAM  Combine cognac, juices, syrup and orange blossom water in a bowl. Take 1 cup of this liquid and warm it in either a saucepan on low for 2 minutes or in the microwave for 20 seconds until slightly warm, not hot. Wring out any extra moisture from the gelatin and dissolve it in the warmed mixture. Add the warmed gelatin mixture to the rest of the liquid and refrigerate for about 2 hours or until the mixture is loosely but not completely set.

Spoon the mixture into a whipped cream dispenser and charge with one cartridge of nitrous oxide. Chill the dispenser for one more hour, then shake very well before dispensing.

FOUR O'CLOCK COCKTAIL  In a mixing glass, dissolve sugar cube in water and bitters. Add bourbon, Grand Marnier and lemon juice. Half-fill the mixing glass with ice and stir until mixing glass is cold to the touch. If necessary, adjust the balance of sweetness and acidity to taste with additional sugar and lemon juice. Strain into a chilled martini glass and top with vanilla citrus foam.

< FOUR O'CLOCK

# m'dear

1 oz Blandy's Duke
of Clarence Madeira

1 oz Giffard Abricot du
Roussillon apricot liqueur

3 dashes Fee Brothers
whiskey barrel-aged bitters

5 drops freshly squeezed lemon juice

This cocktail is meant to be fairly sweet, nutty and a touch bitter, lifted with an ever so slight acidity, and it can be used in place of a dessert wine like Sauternes. Pair with foie gras or rich cheeses.

PLACE all liquid ingredients in a mixing glass half-filled with ice. Gently stir until moderately chilled. If necessary, adjust the acidity to taste with additional lemon juice. Strain into a dessert wine glass and serve.

# noyeau glacé

¼ oz Giffard Ginger
of the Indies ginger liqueur

½ oz 42 Below Manuka honey vodka

½ oz 42 Below vodka

½ oz Giffard Abricot du Roussillon
or other apricot liqueur

½ oz Giffard Crème de Pêches
or other peach liqueur

3 drops freshly squeezed lemon juice

4 dried chamomile flowers

This gentle cocktail subtly captures some of the wonderful flavours of the orchard fruit of British Columbia. A hint of honey glazes the ripe flavours of peach and apricot with a slight spice from ginger. Garnish this drink with dried chamomile flowers, which are available at tea shops.

RINSE the inside of a chilled martini glass with ginger liqueur and discard the excess. Combine honey vodka, regular vodka and apricot and peach liqueurs in a mixing glass and add lemon juice. Fill with ice and shake until mixing glass is cold to the touch. If necessary, adjust the balance of acidity to taste with additional lemon juice. Strain into the rinsed martini glass, then top with chamomile flowers and serve.

# pear-agon

½ pear, perfectly ripe and cored

1½ oz Plymouth Gin
or another premium gin

1 oz Giffard Manzana Verde
or other apple liqueur

½ oz freshly squeezed lime juice

¼ oz simple syrup (page 235)

2 large sprigs fresh tarragon,
plus a small piece for garnish

This cocktail captures the beauty of a pear in an unexpected setting and works well on its own or pairs well with roasted or grilled poultry, scallops or halibut. The forward presence of tarragon in this drink complements the pear flavour, which is balanced with natural sweetness and a slight acidity.

MUDDLE the pear in a mixing glass. Add gin, apple liqueur, lime juice, simple syrup and tarragon. Fill the mixing glass with ice and shake vigorously until the shaker is very cold to the touch. If necessary, adjust the balance of sweetness and acidity to taste with additional syrup and lime juice. Double-strain the cocktail into a chilled martini glass: using a cocktail strainer to hold back most of the pulp, strain through a tea strainer to remove the remaining fine pulp, tapping the strainer to help the liquid pass through. Float a small sprig of tarragon on the surface to garnish.

winter

# the top
# table team

Compared with a mere two decades ago, Vancouver's food scene is virtually unrecognizable. Today, the city

and its environs are home to many ethnic foods and restaurants, and their influences inform any definition

of Pacific Coast cuisine. But not so long ago, fine food was defined here as French onion soup at the big city

hotel of the day. Whistler was, back then, an adjunct of sorts, and that was where, over twenty-five years ago,

Jack Evrensel opened his first restaurant, Araxi. It stands there to this day, on the main square in Whistler

Village, a more focussed, fine-dining experience today than ever. CinCin in Vancouver was next, opening

in 1991, and then both Blue Water Cafe and West opened in 2000. The four restaurants comprise Top Table

Restaurants & Bars. Neil Henderson, in charge of projects for Top Table, says, "All four of our restaurants

are about being hospitable and accommodating." Each, though, is extremely independent of the others and

creates its own culture. The cast of characters who have seen action in these restaurants is in itself a Hall of

Fame roster, while the people currently in place are at the top of their respective fields of expertise.

West, like any fine restaurant, has a long list of alumni. Its name appears, therefore, on many a résumé and is mentioned with professional pride as young chefs pursue their careers. Founding executive chef David Hawksworth, for example, came to West from London, where he had worked with, among others, Marco Pierre White, David Kinch and Stephen Terry. Says Hawksworth, "I knew West was a great opportunity to explore the kind of cooking I wanted to do. The tough part would be finding and sourcing the right ingredients. And then we do as little with them as possible, to make the flavours shine. That is a great challenge. The seasonal mentality wasn't quite there yet in Vancouver, but we were exploring it. And plating, too, something I learned from Phil Howard. West was the perfect place to bring this forward to the Vancouver dining scene."

The response to Hawksworth and West was immediate and resoundingly positive. Under the direction of Brian Hopkins, the restaurant seemed to really take flight. The accolades as Restaurant of the Year from virtually every local publication were augmented by national and international recognition as well—in *Frommer's*, Zagat, *Food and Wine* magazine and *Gourmet*, to name a few. The awards for food, for chef of the year and for service began to pile up, and the influx of accolades has not abated.

Andrew Richardson was part of the triumvirate of chefs that opened what was then Ouest, before moving on to work at The French Laundry, then returning home to Newcastle, England, to revitalize the fine-dining scene there. "I loved working with David and [Pastry Chef] Thierry and Brian at West, and with Jack, both at West and Araxi. The commitment to the best products, and to overall excellence, was there from the time we began to prep for opening." He remembers the opening months very well. "We felt we were breaking new ground; it was all so exciting, although there was a lot of pressure to really take things to the next level." Marc-André Choquette, who became sous chef after Andrew departed, eventually moved on as well, making his name at Lumière and earning industry-wide respect, eventually becoming executive chef at Voya.

The third founding member at Ouest was pastry chef extraordinaire Thierry Busset, whose list of friends in the business includes Gordon Ramsay and Robert Reid. He remembers the first days well: "I would look out into the dining room and watch how people were responding. It went very well for a few months, but I noticed something was not quite right, that not enough people really appreciated what we were doing. I did adapt, of course. I was used to three-star pressure, so it was okay. Vancouver eight years ago was not as ready for this level of cooking. Today, I believe it is. But back then we had to adjust. It was difficult, and I am sure difficult for David in particular. When West came about, I was not really working, and I thought it would be interesting to open that calibre of restaurant in Vancouver." He smiles and says, "Jack's philosophy was good. He gave us everything we needed, placed right in our own hands. That is very important for me. It is not about money; it is about passion for my work." He adds, "It is about working with people who enjoy what they do."

According to Jack, "Blue Water Cafe was three years in the making, in my head, and when we finally found a location and began construction, then changed locations, during that time the idea of West took shape. It did so partly because there were simply too many talented people that wanted to be a part of Blue Water Cafe and its promise. Some of those people opened West." That "promise" has two important facets: Top Table's team members contribute their talent and hard work and know they are part of an organization that strives for the best possible dining experience, night in and night out. And guests of each restaurant will know they will have a great experience every time they dine there. If anything, that is what Top Table, with its four restaurants, actually means.

# risotto of butternut squash and sage

4 cups vegetable oil for deep frying

30 sage leaves

4 cups vegetable stock (page 228)

¼ cup + 2 tsp unsalted butter

4 oz butternut squash, peeled
and cut into ¼-inch dice

1 Tbsp curry powder

1 Tbsp extra-virgin olive oil

½ Spanish onion, finely chopped

1¼ cups Acquarello rice

⅓ cup white wine

⅓ cup grated Parmesan cheese

Juice of 1 lemon

¼ cup whipping cream,
lightly whipped

*Serves 4*

HEAT vegetable oil in a deep fryer or deep pot to 350°F. Add 20 of the sage leaves and fry for 30 seconds. Remove them from the oil with a slotted spoon, allowing them to drain on paper towels, and season with salt. Julienne the remaining 10 sage leaves.

Heat vegetable stock and keep warm.

In a small sauté pan, heat 2 tsp of the butter on medium heat. Add butternut squash and curry powder and sauté for about 10 minutes until soft.

Meanwhile, heat olive oil in a large pot on medium heat. Add onion and cook for 4 to 5 minutes until soft but not browned. Add rice and stir for 2 minutes.

Add wine and cook until wine has completely evaporated, about 3 minutes. While stirring the rice constantly, add stock one ladleful at a time, waiting until each ladleful is absorbed before adding the next one. Cook the rice until it is al dente, about 16 minutes. Remove from heat.

Add butternut squash, Parmesan and julienned sage. Fold in remaining ¼ cup of butter, add lemon juice and season with salt and pepper to taste. Fold in whipped cream.

TO SERVE  Ladle risotto into individual bowls and garnish with fried sage leaves.

SUGGESTED WINE  This is a classic example of when to respect tradition and drink regional wine with regional food. Most dry Italian whites, like good Soave Classico, Chardonnay, falanghina or Gavi di Gavi, will create harmony with this risotto.

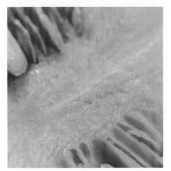

**ON THE WEBSITE** for North Arm Farms in Pemberton, where West sources its butternut squash, you will find a link labelled "seasonal." Click on it, and up comes a list of the produce available there and the time frame for each item's availability. It is a remarkable thing to see, simply because the time frame for everything, from raspberries and asparagus through potatoes and carrots, is so very short. When a restaurant commits to using seasonal and local ingredients, it is no small matter. Sourcing is one of the biggest challenges, along with maintaining fresh ingredients year-round, especially over the winter.

Butternut squash usually makes its way to market in early October. It is picked from its vine in a mature state, and the rind is allowed to harden for storage purposes. Native to Mexico, it has a history as a food staple, along with maize and beans, of nearly five thousand years. Its relatives include zucchini, cucumber and pumpkin—in fact, it is known as butternut pumpkin in Australia. The flavour is remarkably similar to pumpkin—nutty, a touch spicy. It is a quintessential winter ingredient embodying the warmth, heartiness and rich flavours that we savour so much because they are vital in fending off that cold, cold night.

# butternut squash

# seared scallops with
# butternut squash remoulade

1 large butternut squash, 1½–2 lbs

1 tsp Moutarde de Meaux

¼ cup + 4 tsp olive oil

½ tsp chardonnay vinegar

½ oz cilantro, julienned
(about 1 Tbsp)

½ cup chicken stock (page 231)

3 Tbsp unsalted butter

2 tsp whipping cream

2 sprigs thyme

12 medium scallops,
1½ lbs total

4 sprigs chervil, for garnish

*Serves 4*

This recipe calls for Moutarde de Meaux, a light, whole-grain mustard, and chardonnay vinegar. If you cannot find chardonnay vinegar, substitute with a relatively sweet white or cider vinegar.

REMOVE skin from butternut squash and separate the neck from the bulb. Cut half of the neck into twelve ¼-inch slices, then use a 1½-inch cutter to cut out discs. Julienne the other half of the neck and lightly salt. After 8 to 10 minutes, drain the liquid and add mustard, ¼ cup of the olive oil, chardonnay vinegar and cilantro.

Remove the seeds from the bulb and dice the flesh. Place the flesh in a medium saucepan with chicken stock and 1 Tbsp of the butter, and season with salt and pepper. Bring to a boil and simmer until tender, about 10 minutes. Purée in a blender, then pass through a fine sieve. Hang the purée in a cheesecloth, retaining both the liquid and the solids.

To ½ cup of the liquid, add the cream and 2 tsp of the butter. Season with salt and pepper.

In a medium pan, heat 2 tsp of the olive oil and the remaining 4 tsp of butter on medium heat. When the butter browns and emits a nutty aroma, add thyme and butternut discs and cook discs for 3 to 4 minutes until golden.

Preheat the oven to 350°F. Heat an ovenproof, non-stick pan on high heat. Add the remaining 2 tsp of olive oil, then add scallops. Place the pan in the oven and roast for 2 to 3 minutes.

TO SERVE  In the centre of each of four plates, spoon about 2 tsp of the butternut squash purée, then gently tap the plates so that the purée settles into a circle. Place a quarter of the remoulade in the centre and fan out three butternut squash discs on top. Arrange three scallops around the purée.

Whisk the butternut squash–cream mixture to produce a light foam, and spoon this foam around the plate. Garnish with a sprig of chervil.

SUGGESTED WINE  Pair this dish with medium- to full-bodied whites with a richness to balance the sweet scallops and the savoury squash. A nice B.C. chardonnay would be fabulous, and for an unoaked option try a lush Alsace pinot gris.

# quail ravioli with onion velouté

### QUAIL RAVIOLI

4 oz chicken breast, cubed

1 egg white

6 Tbsp whipping cream

2 Tbsp extra-virgin olive oil

8 oz mixed mushrooms

2 shallots, finely minced

1 tsp truffle oil

4 cups chicken stock (page 231)

Breasts from 2 whole jumbo quails

12 oz pasta dough (page 237)

1 tsp semolina flour for dusting

### QUAIL JUS

Bones from 2 jumbo quails,
chopped into 2-inch pieces

¼ cup extra-virgin olive oil

4 oz button mushrooms, sliced

3 shallots, sliced

1 clove garlic, crushed

1 sprig thyme

2 bay leaves

2 Tbsp sherry vinegar

⅓ cup Madeira

⅓ cup red wine

2 Tbsp whipping cream

4 cups poaching liquid
from quail ravioli

*Serves 4*

Morels, chanterelles and porcinis would be great mushrooms for this dish—they seem to go hand in hand with quail. This recipe takes two whole quails. Ask your butcher to separate the breasts from the bones; you'll need the former for the ravioli and the latter for the sauce.

QUAIL RAVIOLI Blend chicken and egg white in a food processor. Slowly add 3 Tbsp of the cream. Pass this chicken purée through a very fine tamis, using a plastic scraper. Place the purée into a bowl over ice and fold in the remaining 3 Tbsp of cream.

In a small sauté pan, heat 2 tsp of the olive oil on high heat. Add mushrooms and sauté for about 4 minutes. Drain off excess moisture and remove the mushrooms from the pan. Heat the remaining 4 tsp of olive oil on medium heat. Add mushrooms and shallots and sauté until soft but not browned, about 2 minutes. Chop the mushrooms into small dice and add to the chicken mousse, along with truffle oil. Season with salt and pepper.

Bring stock to a boil. Add quail and poach for 1 minute. Remove from the stock and allow to cool. Reserve 4 cups of poaching liquid for quail jus.

Roll out the pasta dough on the lowest setting on a pasta maker or to the thickness of a dime. Cut into eight discs, each 4 inches in diameter.

Dust a baking sheet with semolina flour.

Spread a quarter of the chicken and mushroom farce on each quail breast.

Place each quail breast on a round of pasta and cover with another round. Press edges together to seal, making sure to smooth out any air pockets. Keep on the floured baking sheet until ready to serve.

QUAIL JUS Preheat the oven to 500°F. Place bones in a shallow baking dish. Roast bones in the oven for 30 minutes or until golden brown, stirring every 10 minutes.

## ONION VELOUTÉ

2 Tbsp unsalted butter

1 onion, thinly sliced

1 sprig thyme, leaves picked off and stem discarded

¾ cup whole milk

## CHANTERELLE GARNISH

2 Tbsp unsalted butter

8 oz golden chanterelle mushrooms, quartered

In a large saucepan, heat olive oil on medium heat. Add mushrooms, shallots and garlic and sweat until soft but not browned, about 8 minutes. Add thyme and bay leaves. Add roasted bones and deglaze the saucepan with vinegar, Madeira and red wine. Add whipping cream, then cook until liquid has reduced by three-quarters, about 10 minutes. Add poaching liquid. Simmer for 1½ hours, skimming impurities off the surface every 15 minutes or so. Strain the jus through a fine sieve, discarding the solids, and simmer the jus for about 20 minutes to reduce to a sauce.

ONION VELOUTÉ  Heat butter on medium heat in a medium saucepan. Add onion and thyme. Cover with milk and simmer for 25 minutes. Purée in a blender and pass the mixture through a fine sieve.

CHANTERELLE GARNISH  In a small saucepan, heat butter on medium heat. Add chanterelles and sauté until they are cooked, about 3 minutes.

TO SERVE  Warm both the onion velouté and the quail jus. Bring a large pot of salted water to a boil. Add ravioli and cook for 4 minutes.

Spoon a quarter of the chanterelles into each of four bowls. Put one raviolo on top. Drizzle with about 2 Tbsp of jus and pour a quarter of the onion velouté overtop.

SUGGESTED WINE  Try an elegant, well-structured, earthy red like Rioja reserva, Brunello or Cannonau.

ABOVE: quail ravioli with onion velouté

RIGHT: galantine of quail, foie gras and jasmine-poached raisins

# galantine of quail, foie gras and jasmine-poached raisins

**FOIE GRAS PARFAIT**

5 tsp port

5 tsp Madeira

2 tsp brandy

1 shallot, sliced

1 sprig thyme

1 clove garlic, sliced

2 oz fresh chicken livers, warmed to room temperature

2 oz foie gras, warmed to room temperature

1 egg, lightly beaten

⅓ cup unsalted butter, melted

**JASMINE-POACHED RAISINS**

¼ cup sweet wine, like Essensia orange muscat

⅓ cup water

⅓ cup raisins, washed

Pinch of Chinese five-spice powder

1 tsp jasmine tea leaves, bundled in a cheesecloth

*Serves 4*

**FOIE GRAS PARFAIT** In a small saucepan, combine port, Madeira, brandy, shallot, thyme and garlic and cook on medium heat until liquid is reduced to 1 Tbsp. Strain this reduction through a sieve and discard the solids.

Place chicken livers and foie gras in a blender, add reduction and blend until smooth, about 2 minutes. Add egg slowly while continuing to blend. Then add melted butter and salt and pepper. Pass this parfait through a fine sieve and chill in the refrigerator until cold.

**JASMINE-POACHED RAISINS** In a small saucepan, combine wine with water and bring to a boil. Add raisins, five-spice powder and tea. Simmer for 5 minutes, remove from heat and allow to stand for 1 hour.

Remove 3 Tbsp of the raisins and set them aside in the refrigerator. Remove and discard the tea leaves, then place the liquid and remaining raisins in a blender and blend until smooth. Pass this raisin mixture through a fine sieve and chill in the refrigerator until cold.

**FOIE GRAS** Remove and discard any veins and blood clots from the foie gras and place the foie gras into a bowl. Add salt, sugar, five-spice powder, sweet wine, port and brandy and allow to marinate for 6 hours.

Preheat the oven to 275°F.

Place the foie gras into a small rectangular ovenproof pan. Place this pan in a baking dish. Pour boiling water into the baking dish around the pan to make a bain marie, then place the baking dish in the oven and cook for 9 minutes. Remove from oven and allow to set in the refrigerator for 12 hours.

Cut foie gras into twelve batons about 1¼ inches in length.

## FOIE GRAS

4 oz foie gras, warmed
to room temperature

½ tsp salt

½ tsp sugar

Pinch of Chinese
five-spice powder

2 tsp sweet wine, like
Essensia orange muscat

2 tsp white port

1 tsp brandy

## QUAIL GALANTINE

4 tsp jasmine-poached raisins

4 tsp foie gras parfait

4 quails, 5 oz each, deboned,
with skin between breasts
intact and legs separated

2 tsp olive oil

1 oz mixed cress leaves,
for garnish

QUAIL GALANTINE  Mix jasmine-poached raisins with foie gras parfait in a bowl.

Lay each quail skin-side down on a piece of plastic wrap about 16 inches × 8 inches. Season the flesh with salt and pepper, then spoon 2 tsp of the parfait and raisin mixture into the centre of the quail. Use the plastic wrap to fold the quail breasts over the filling to form a sausage shape roughly 2¼ inches in diameter. Tie the ends of the plastic wrap to secure.

Steam the quail for 9 minutes, then allow it to cool in the fridge for at least 4 hours (overnight is best).

Heat olive oil in a medium sauté pan on high heat. Add quail legs and roast them for 4 minutes per side.

TO SERVE  On each of four plates, smear 2 tsp of raisin purée in a ring, following the contour of the plate. Cut each quail into four even slices and fan them out on the plate. Rest a roasted leg on the breast meat. Sprinkle the reserved raisins and three batons of foie gras around each plate. Sprinkle cress leaves overtop of the quail.

SUGGESTED WINE  A white with a little residual sugar would complement the rich foie gras and would have the sweetness to stand up to the jasmine-poached raisins. Try a moelleux Vouvray or a rich gewürztraminer from Alsace.

# west bacon with roasted scallops and tomato relish

½ cup sugar

⅓ cup red wine vinegar

2 Tbsp extra-virgin olive oil

½ red onion, minced

2 cloves garlic, minced

2½ oz ginger, grated

1 jalapeño, deseeded and finely diced

10 tomatoes concassé (page 237)

⅓ cup tomato paste

½ tsp mustard seeds

½ tsp black peppercorns

½ tsp cardamom seeds

½ tsp red chili flakes

1 pod star anise

3 cloves

*Serves 4*

Any fresh, large scallops would work for this recipe, but weathervane scallops are the best, since they are usually very large and sweet and are of exceptional quality.

TOMATO RELISH Place the sugar in a heavy-bottomed saucepan on medium heat. Stir frequently and watch that the caramel doesn't burn. When the caramel is light brown, 3 to 4 minutes, carefully pour in the red wine vinegar and stir to dissolve the sugar. Reduce for 3 minutes to create a gastrique with a sweet-and-sour flavour.

Heat olive oil in a medium sauté pan on medium heat. Add onion, garlic, ginger and jalapeño and sweat until soft but not browned, about 10 minutes. Add tomatoes and tomato paste. Add the gastrique.

In a heavy-bottomed sauté pan, toast mustard seeds, black peppercorns, cardamom, red chili flakes, star anise and cloves on high heat for about 2 minutes. Crush the spices and add to the tomato mixture.

Cook the tomato mixture on medium heat for 1 hour, stirring every 10 minutes or so, until the mixture has the consistency of jam.

BACON AND SCALLOPS Heat fennel seeds, coriander seeds, cardamom, star anise and cloves in a heavy-bottomed sauté pan on medium heat for about 3 minutes to toast the spices. Crush the spices and mix with the brown sugar and kosher salt.

Generously spread this spice rub on the pork and allow it to sit at room temperature for 12 hours. Rinse the rub from the pork and pat dry with a paper towel.

Roll pork into a roast and tie tightly with kitchen string.

BACON AND SCALLOPS

2 Tbsp fennel seeds

2 Tbsp coriander seeds

2 Tbsp cardamom

1 pod star anise

1 Tbsp cloves

¾ cup brown sugar, gently packed

1¼ cups kosher salt

2 lbs pork belly, skin removed
and all fat trimmed off

¼ cup + 4 tsp olive oil

1 carrot, sliced

2 ribs celery, sliced

1 Spanish onion, sliced

1 clove garlic, crushed

1 sprig thyme

1 bay leaf

8 large scallops

2 oz micro greens

2 tsp citrus dressing (page 236)

Preheat the oven to 325°F. Heat 4 tsp of the olive oil in a large ovenproof pan on medium heat. Add pork and sear for about 5 minutes on each side, being careful not to burn the meat.

Remove pork from the pan. Add carrot, celery, onion, garlic, thyme and bay leaf to the pan. Sweat until soft but not browned, about 15 minutes.

Put the pork back in the pan and cover the entire roll with water. Place in the oven and braise for 3 hours until pork is soft to the touch.

Remove the pork from the liquid and allow it to rest for about 20 minutes, uncovered. While the pork is still slightly warm, roll it very tightly in several layers of plastic wrap, tying the ends to seal.

Refrigerate overnight, about 12 hours.

Preheat the oven to 400°F. Cut pork into slices 1 inch thick. In a medium ovenproof sauté pan, heat 2 Tbsp of the olive oil on medium heat. Sear pork slices for 3 minutes on each side. Remove from heat and spread a layer of tomato relish on top. Place in the oven for 5 minutes until the pork slices are warmed through.

Heat the remaining 2 Tbsp of olive oil in a small sauté pan on medium heat. Add scallops and sear for 1 minute on each side.

In a small bowl, toss micro greens with citrus dressing.

TO SERVE  On the middle of each of four plates, place a slice of pork. Top with two scallops and garnish with a quarter of the micro greens.

SUGGESTED WINE  Try a German kabinett or spätlese riesling from the Mosel or Rheingau.

# roasted celeriac risotto
## with shaved black winter truffles

1 small celeriac, about 8 oz, peeled and cut into ½-inch dice, peel discarded but trimmings reserved

7 Tbsp unsalted butter

2 cups chicken stock (page 231)

2 tsp olive oil

¼ onion, finely chopped

1 clove garlic, chopped

1 sprig thyme

1 bay leaf

1 cup biodynamic arborio rice

¼ cup white wine

¼ cup acid butter (page 235)

2 oz Parmigiano-Reggiano, grated (about ¼ cup)

Deep-fried parsley for garnish (page 237)

½ oz winter truffle (Périgord)

*Serves 4*

Fresh winter truffles come from the Périgord region of France and are heavily scented. The strength of the truffles' flavour is essential to this dish. Cheaper alternatives are available in jars, but they suffer from a serious lack of flavour.

FINELY chop all the celeriac trimmings. In a small sauté pan, heat 3 Tbsp of the butter on medium heat until it browns and emits a nutty scent. Add celeriac trimmings and sauté for 15 to 18 minutes. Moisten with ¼ cup of the chicken stock. Purée this mixture in a blender, pass through a fine sieve and season with salt and pepper.

Heat 4 tsp of the butter in a small sauté pan on medium heat. Add celeriac dice and sauté 10 to 12 minutes until brown. Drain and set aside.

In a large, heavy-bottomed saucepan, heat olive oil and 2 tsp of the butter on medium heat. Add onion, garlic, thyme and bay leaf and cook for 4 to 5 minutes, until vegetables are soft. Add rice and gently stir until grains take on a glassy look.

Add wine and cook until the liquid has totally evaporated and grains are not stuck together. Add 1½ cups of the chicken stock, ¼ cup at a time, stirring between additions until all of the liquid is absorbed. Fold in 4 tsp of the celeriac purée and all of the celeriac dice. Add the remaining 6 tsp of the butter, acid butter and Parmigiano-Reggiano. Loosen the risotto with remaining stock if it is too thick.

TO SERVE Ladle a quarter of the risotto onto each of four flat plates. Garnish with fried parsley. At the table, finely shave a quarter of the truffle over each serving.

SUGGESTED WINE For the true wine-and-truffle experience, you need to open an aged bottle of barolo, the king of Italian wines.

LEFT: rump of beef with cromesquis of oxtail and foie gras, roasted red onions and confit portobello mushrooms
BELOW: beef strip loin with fricassée of porcinis and bacon with pommes purée

# beef strip loin with fricassée of porcinis and bacon with pommes purée

½ cup + 3 Tbsp olive oil

2 shallots, peeled and sliced

4 sprigs thyme

1 bay leaf

⅓ cup red wine

⅓ cup port

¾ cup brown veal and chicken jus (page 232)

¾ cup cold butter, cut into ½-inch dice

3 russet potatoes, peeled and quartered

⅓ cup whipping cream

4 pieces beef strip loin, 6 oz each

20 pearl onions, peeled

½ cup bacon lardons, cut into pieces ¼ inch × ¼ inch × ½ inch

½ lb fresh porcini mushrooms, cleaned and cut into large pieces

10 parsley leaves, chopped

*Serves 4*

This recipe uses the sous-vide technique, in which the beef is vacuum-sealed in a bag and then gently cooked at a low temperature. This method results in incredibly tender and flavourful meat. If you do not have a vacuum sealer and vacuum bags, just roast the beef in a pan in the oven the conventional way: season the beef, heat one tablespoon of olive oil in an ovenproof sauté pan on high heat, add the beef and sear until golden all over, about 1 minute on each side. Add one tablespoon of butter, roast in a 350°F oven for 5 minutes and remove it from the oven. Baste the meat for 1 minute, then allow it to rest for 10 minutes more.

IN a small saucepan, heat 2 Tbsp olive oil with shallots, 2 sprigs of thyme and bay leaf on low heat and cook until shallots are translucent. Deglaze the pan with wine and port and continue cooking until liquid has reduced to a syrup, about 25 minutes. Add jus and simmer slowly for 1½ hours. Strain the liquid through a sieve into a small saucepan and heat on medium heat until the sauce sticks to the back of a spoon, about 10 minutes. Whisk in 2 cubes of butter and set aside.

Place potatoes in a medium pot and cover with cold salted water. Bring to a boil on high heat. Reduce heat to medium and cook until a toothpick easily pierces the potatoes, about 15 minutes, making sure not to overcook them. Drain the potatoes, then allow them to sit and evaporate for a further 1 minute. Pass the potatoes through a tamis into a medium mixing bowl. Place potatoes back in the pan, fold in cream and ¼ cup of the butter, softening the potato with a spatula. Incorporate 2 more Tbsp of butter and pass again through a fine tamis, using a plastic pastry scraper. Adjust seasoning with salt and pepper. Set aside.

Place each piece of beef strip loin in a vacuum-sealable bag. Add thyme and a cube of butter. Evacuate the bag on a medium vacuum.

Heat a large pot of water to 145°F, using a thermometer to check the temperature. Submerge the vacuum-sealed bags in the water for 25 minutes, then remove the bags, cut them open, and season the beef with salt and pepper. In a heavy-bottomed sauté pan, heat 3 Tbsp of the olive oil on high heat, add the beef and sear for 3 minutes on each side. Add the remaining butter and baste the meat for 5 minutes, rotating the beef from time to time. Allow it to rest for at least 5 minutes. The beef should be medium rare.

In a heavy-bottomed pan, heat 2 Tbsp olive oil on medium heat. Add onions and roast for about 10 minutes until golden brown and well caramelized. Turn the onions from time to time to ensure all sides cook evenly.

In a small sauté pan, heat 2 Tbsp olive oil on high heat. Add bacon lardons and roast until crisp, about 4 minutes.

In a separate pan, heat 1 Tbsp olive oil on high heat. Add the mushrooms and roast until golden brown, 4 or 5 minutes. Add the onions, bacon and parsley. Adjust seasoning with salt and pepper.

TO SERVE Reheat the potato purée on low heat. Scoop a quarter of the purée onto each of four plates. Spoon a quarter of the mushroom, onion and bacon ragout beside the potatoes. Cut each portion of beef in half and place on the mushroom ragout. Finish the dish with a drizzle of the jus.

SUGGESTED WINE A rustic earthy red would work well with woodsy porcini; try something from southern Rhône, like Gigondas or Vacqueyras. The dark, dense structured Malbecs from Mendoza, Argentina, would also be grand.

# brined, smoked and roasted chicken

**ROAST CHICKEN**

4 cups water

½ cup kosher salt

1 sprig tarragon

1 Tbsp jasmine tea leaves

10 black peppercorns

2 whole chickens,
wings and legs removed

2 Tbsp olive oil

**ARTICHOKE PURÉE**

2 Tbsp olive oil

1 carrot, sliced

½ onion, sliced

2 cloves garlic, crushed

½ bulb fennel, sliced

3 medium artichokes, outer leaves
trimmed, halved and choke removed

½ cup white wine

½ cup chicken stock (page 231)

*Serves 4*

The smoking procedure described in this recipe is a good way of smoking foods if you don't have the luxury of a smoking box. You will need two handfuls of charcoal and a handful of mesquite wood chips. You will also need a large, solid steel container with a lid and a wire insert like a grill that will hold the chicken above the smouldering wood chips. This method is known as a cold smoke, as it imparts a smoky flavour to foods without cooking them.

ROAST CHICKEN   In a large pot, make a brine by bringing water, salt, tarragon, tea leaves and black peppercorns to a boil. Remove from heat and allow to cool completely. Place chicken crowns in the brine and let them sit in the refrigerator for 2 hours.

Preheat the oven to 400°F. Place the charcoal in the oven and allow it to get extremely hot. Remove from the oven and ignite the charcoal with a kitchen torch. Transfer the charcoal to the steel container. While the charcoal is red hot, pour wood chips on top. Place the chickens on the grill. Cover and allow to smoke for 30 minutes.

In a large, ovenproof sauté pan, heat olive oil on medium heat. Add chickens and sear, breast-side down, about 5 minutes to crisp the skin. Turn chicken crowns over and put the pan in the oven for 10 minutes or until chicken is cooked but still moist. Allow to rest for 5 minutes, then carve off the breasts and set them aside.

ARTICHOKE PURÉE   Heat olive oil in a medium sauté pan on medium heat. Add carrot, onion, garlic and fennel and sauté for about 5 minutes, until softened and lightly golden. Add artichokes. Add wine and stock, then season with salt and pepper. Bring to a simmer, then cook until artichokes are soft, about 30 minutes.

## ASPARAGUS AND ARTICHOKE SALAD

4 spears asparagus

1 artichoke, outer leaves trimmed, halved and choke removed

4 tsp citrus dressing (page 236)

In a blender, combine artichokes with ⅓ cup of the cooking liquid. Purée and season to taste with salt and pepper.

ASPARAGUS AND ARTICHOKE SALAD  Trim the woody ends from the asparagus. Using a vegetable peeler, shave the asparagus into thin strips. Slice artichoke into thin slices (about ⅛ inch thick) with a mandolin. Toss together with citrus dressing.

TO SERVE  In the middle of each of four plates, spoon a quarter of the artichoke purée. Place a chicken breast on top and finish with the asparagus and artichoke salad.

SUGGESTED WINE  The smokiness of this dish would be well complemented by rich, oaked whites such as Meursault or good California chardonnays.

# red wine–poached sablefish with
# manila clams and smoked streaky bacon

12 very thin slices of bacon

1 carrot, cut into ⅛-inch strips

¼ head Savoy cabbage,
coarsely diced

⅓ cup fish velouté (page 230)

20 Manila clams

1 Tbsp grainy mustard

½ oz chives, chopped
(about 2 Tbsp)

Juice of 1 lemon

3 cups red wine

1 sprig thyme

1 pod star anise

10 black peppercorns

4 fillets sablefish, 5 oz each

*Serves 4*

LINE a baking sheet with parchment paper and preheat the oven to 300°F.

Lay out bacon slices on the baking sheet. Top with another piece of parchment and another baking sheet. Place in the oven and cook for 30 minutes.

Bring a medium pot of water to a boil. Add carrot and cabbage and blanch for about 1 minute or until just cooked. Remove from the water and set aside.

In a medium pot, bring the fish velouté and clams to a simmer and cook until the clams open, about 5 minutes. Add carrots and cabbage, then add mustard and chives. Season with lemon juice and kosher salt to taste.

In a large saucepan, combine wine, thyme, star anise and black peppercorns. Cook on medium heat until reduced by half, about 10 minutes. Add sablefish and cook in simmering wine, uncovered, for about 7 minutes. Remove the fish from the wine.

TO SERVE  On each of four plates, lay out three slices of bacon. Spoon a quarter of the clams, vegetables and fish velouté onto the middle of each plate. Top with a fillet of fish.

SUGGESTED WINE  A light- to medium-bodied red with softer ripe fruit and low tannin content would work well with this dish—try Santa Barbara pinot noir or Valpolicella.

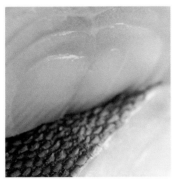

**THIS FISH,** sometimes called black cod though it is not a cod at all, has an oily meat rich in Omega-3 fatty acids, and its delicate flavour and large, velvety flakes make it ideal for Asian-based dishes. The Japanese, in fact, harvested sablefish by long-range vessels from the Pacific Northwest until 1977, when Canada established its two-hundred-mile international fisheries boundary. Up to that point, sablefish was considered strictly a bycatch fish here, sold for little money and often actually discarded. The boundary meant that the Japanese had to buy Canadian sablefish rather than catch it for themselves, and this demand created a now-lucrative, highly regulated market with a vessel-by-vessel quota and a maximum total production of about four thousand tonnes (9 million pounds) per year.

Sablefish has enjoyed a recent surge of popularity as the North American palate evolved to appreciate it and environmental consciousness began to dictate our eating habits—Canadian Pacific sablefish is considered a sustainable species. West has been cooking with it pretty much since day one. It can be hot-smoked, in which case it requires further cooking, or it can be prepared fresh. Roasting and poaching seem to be the favoured methods, and even a smoky bacon accompaniment can work well. The catch that appears at West is long-line caught and frozen at sea so that the fish is optimal when the chefs prepare it at the restaurant. And we do mean long lines: sablefish prefer waters off the northwest coast of Vancouver Island of depths ranging from six hundred to four thousand feet.

# sablefish

OPPOSITE PAGE: sablefish in curry butter
with sunchoke purée and roasted pearl onions

# honey and black pepper–roasted duck breast
# with crisp confit and spiced duck consommé

2 egg whites

1 carrot, minced

2 ribs celery, minced

⅛ onion, minced

3½ oz chicken breast, minced

DUCK CONFIT,
BREASTS AND CONSOMMÉ

2 cups duck fat

2 whole ducks, 3½–4 lbs,
legs removed and lightly
seasoned 24 hours in advance

2 Tbsp vegetable oil

2 carrots, chopped

2 ribs celery, chopped

1 onion, chopped

1 clove garlic, chopped

Pinch of ground cumin

Pinch of ground ginger

Pinch of caraway seeds

Pinch of coriander seeds

Pinch of ground star anise

1 portion clarification

¼ cup dark honey

2 Tbsp cracked black pepper

Zest of 1 orange, finely grated

*Serves 4*

This recipe calls for dark honey—buckwheat honey is a good example—which is higher in antioxidants than lighter-coloured honeys.

CLARIFICATION  In a small bowl, gently whisk egg whites. Add carrot, celery, onion and chicken breast.

DUCK CONFIT, BREASTS AND CONSOMMÉ  Preheat the oven to 225°F.

In an ovenproof pan, gently warm the duck fat. Wash the seasoning off the duck legs, pat them dry, then add them to the duck fat. Cover and cook in the oven for 2 to 3 hours until tender. Remove the legs from the fat and and allow them to set in the fridge, skin-side down. When set, trim the legs to a drumstick shape.

Remove the breasts from the duck and lightly score the skin. Refrigerate until needed.

Chop the duck carcass into 2-inch pieces. Heat oil in a heavy-bottomed pan on high heat. Add duck bones and roast for 6 to 8 minutes until brown. Add carrots, celery, onion, garlic, cumin, ginger, caraway seeds, coriander seeds and star anise, and roast until vegetables are slightly browned, about 5 minutes. Cover with water, bring to a boil and simmer for 2 hours. Strain the stock through a fine sieve and chill.

Whisk the clarification into the cold stock, place on medium heat and stir gently until a pad forms on top of stock. Break a small hole in the pad to allow the stock to move and simmer gently for 45 minutes. Strain the stock carefully through a cheesecloth and season with salt.

In a small saucepan, bring honey to a boil. Add pepper and orange zest. Remove from heat and allow to cool.

Preheat the oven to 350°F.

2 heads bok choy, 3½ oz each, cored

2 tsp olive oil

2 tsp pickled ginger

1 clove garlic, sliced

1 red chili, finely julienned

Heat a medium, ovenproof sauté pan on high heat. Add duck breasts, skin-side down, and cook for 3 to 4 minutes, allowing fat to render and the skin to brown. Turn the breasts over and sear the flesh side for 1 minute, then roast in the oven, skin-side down, for 5 to 6 minutes. Remove from the oven, turn the breasts over and add honey mixture. Baste on the stove on medium heat for 2 minutes, then allow to rest.

Heat an ovenproof non-stick pan on high heat. Add duck legs, skin-side down, and roast for 8 to 9 minutes in the oven.

STIR-FRIED BOK CHOY Bring a large pot of salted water to a boil. Add bok choy and blanch for 90 seconds, then plunge it into an ice bath to refresh. Break off and dry the leaves.

In a medium sauté pan, heat olive oil on medium heat. Add ginger, garlic and chili and stir for 30 seconds to aromatize. Add bok choy leaves and sauté gently for 1 to 2 minutes. Season with salt and pepper.

TO SERVE In the centre of each of four bowls, arrange bok choy in a 2½-inch ring mould. Remove the mould and place a confit duck leg on top. Cut the breast in half lengthwise, then cut each piece thrice to get six equal pieces. Arrange these duck pieces around the bowl. Ladle a quarter of the consommé into each bowl.

SUGGESTED WINE A floral, lightly off-dry white will cool the heat of the black pepper and spice. Gewürztraminers from Alsace, with their distinctive aromas of rose petals and lychees and a soft rich palate, are perfect with this dish. If you love sherry, try a medium-dry amontillado—its fortification gives it enough body to hold up to the flavourful broth.

# vanilla cheesecake with honey-roasted grapefruit, pineapple, oat crisp and grapefruit espuma

### VANILLA CHEESECAKE

1 cup cream cheese, cold

¼ cup sugar

1 egg

¼ cup sour cream

1 tsp vanilla extract

### CRUSHED PINEAPPLE

¼ pineapple, roughly cubed

¼ cup sugar

¼ vanilla bean, seeds scraped out and pod discarded

### OAT CRISP

1 cup rolled oats

¼ cup brown sugar

¼ cup cake flour

¼ cup cold unsalted butter, cubed

¼ tsp baking powder

*Serves 6*

You will need a whipped cream dispenser, available at kitchen supply stores, to make the espuma, but the dessert will still be tasty without it.

VANILLA CHEESECAKE  Grease and dust with sugar six 2½-inch ramekins and preheat the oven to 325°F.

In the bowl of an electric mixer with paddle attachment, cream together cream cheese and sugar. Add egg, then scrape down the sides of the bowl and continue mixing. Add sour cream and vanilla and mix for 10 seconds. Pour batter into the ramekins and place ramekins into a roasting pan. Add water to the pan until the water level reaches about halfway up the ramekins.

Bake in the oven for about 45 minutes, or until the cheesecakes have slightly souffléed but are not browned and a toothpick stuck in the centre of the cake comes out clean.

Allow cheesecakes to cool and chill for 1 hour.

CRUSHED PINEAPPLE  In a blender or food processor, pulse together pineapple, sugar and vanilla until well mixed but still a bit chunky.

OAT CRISP  In the bowl of an electric mixer, combine all ingredients and mix with a paddle attachment until the mixture resembles a coarse meal. Press about 2 Tbsp of this mixture into a 2½-inch ring mould, then remove the mould. Repeat to get six rounds.

Place on a baking sheet and chill in the refrigerator for about 10 minutes, uncovered. Meanwhile, preheat the oven to 350°F.

Bake the crisps until golden brown, about 15 minutes.

3 gelatin leaves, softened
in a bowl of cold water

1 cup grapefruit juice, strained

2½ Tbsp simple syrup (page 235)

HONEY-ROASTED GRAPEFRUIT

2 grapefruits

¼ cup honey

GRAPEFRUIT ESPUMA  Wring extra moisture out of gelatin leaves and place them in a medium stainless-steel bowl. Add ½ cup of the juice and place the bowl over a pot of gently simmering water, stirring to dissolve the gelatin. Remove from heat and add the remaining ½ cup of juice and the syrup. Chill in the refrigerator for 1 hour.

Pour this mixture into a whipped cream dispenser and load with two nitrous oxide cartridges.

HONEY-ROASTED GRAPEFRUIT  Preheat the oven to 350°F.

Using a sharp knife, cut the peel off the grapefruits and cut out the segments between the membranes. Gently toss the segments in a bowl with honey until they are coated. Transfer to a metal baking dish and roast in the oven for about 15 minutes, or until the segments are heated through.

TO SERVE  Run a flat knife along the sides of the ramekins and unmould the cheesecakes.

In the middle of each of six plates, spoon a sixth of the crushed pineapple. Place an oat crisp on top. Place a cheesecake on top of the oat crisp and top with two to three segments of grapefruit. Finish with a dollop of espuma.

SUGGESTED WINE  The high acidity of the citrus can leave many wines feeling fat and flabby. Meet the acidity with B.C. bubbles or harmonize the flavour with a New Zealand sauvignon blanc.

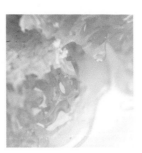

APICULTURE IS ALIVE and well in North America. Bees tap approximately two million flowers in order to produce a pound of honey and fly an astonishing thirty-one-thousand-plus miles during their eight-week life span. Honey has been used as a sweetener for millennia, and in these days of health-conscious and sustainable foods, honey is experiencing something of a fashionable comeback. Honey is harvested from July through September, but because it is a supersaturated sugar solution with antiseptic properties, it is in essence a preserve and is therefore available year-round; its warm sweetness can be enjoyed even in the dead of winter.

Hippocrates used it for various ailments, and he was certainly on to something—honey is now known to have a host of medicinal benefits owing to its high levels of antioxidants and anti-allergens. Best of all, it tastes great. Honey contains traces of substances that are yet to be scientifically identified and therefore cannot be synthetically replicated. It is in some ways a superfood—all natural, packing a long list of desirable vitamins and enzymes, without many of the negative effects of artificial sweeteners or refined sugar.

Bees—and their vital role in pollination—have received a lot of media and scientific attention of late; humans are only beginning to acknowledge how much we depend on these busy creatures and how much our activities have put their survival in jeopardy. This shift in attitude has only made it easier to be grateful for the intensely satisfying flavour of honey-roasted grapefruit adorning a vanilla cheesecake.

# honey

saffron-spiced pumpkin panna cotta
with ginger cake and orange saffron syrup

# saffron-spiced pumpkin panna cotta
# with ginger cake and orange saffron syrup

### PUMPKIN PURÉE

1 small sugar pumpkin, about 2¼ lbs, cut in half and pulp and seeds removed

### PUMPKIN PANNA COTTA

½ cup whole milk

¼ cup whipping cream

⅓ cup pumpkin purée

4 tsp brown sugar

4 tsp granulated sugar

2 cloves

¼ tsp allspice powder

¼ vanilla bean, split and scraped, but pod reserved

Pinch of saffron

2 gelatin leaves, softened in a little cold water

½ oz candied ginger, finely diced (about 1 tsp)

### GINGER CAKE

1½ cups boiling water

¼ cup molasses

¾ cup honey

⅓ cup corn syrup

1 tsp baking soda

*Serves 4*

PUMPKIN PURÉE  Preheat the oven to 350°F. Place pumpkin, cut-side down, on a baking sheet and bake until tender, about 1 hour. Scrape out the pumpkin flesh, purée in a blender and pass through a sieve.

PUMPKIN PANNA COTTA  Lightly grease four 2½-inch ramekins. In a medium saucepan, combine all ingredients except gelatin and candied ginger. Bring to a simmer and cook for 2 minutes. Remove from heat and remove and discard the vanilla pod. Wring the gelatin to remove excess moisture and dissolve it in the pumpkin mixture. Allow the mixture to infuse for 30 minutes. Strain through a fine sieve, then pour into the ramekins.

Chill in the refrigerator for about 3 hours.

GINGER CAKE  Preheat the oven to 350°F. In a small bowl, combine water, molasses, honey, corn syrup and baking soda. In a medium bowl, sift together flour, baking powder, ginger, cinnamon and salt.

In the bowl of an electric mixer with paddle attachment, cream together butter and sugars until the mixture becomes pale in colour. Add egg while continuing to mix. Add a third of the dry ingredients, followed by half of the molasses mixture. Continue to alternate adding dry ingredients and the molasses mixture until all ingredients have been incorporated.

Scrape down the sides of the bowl and mix for another 30 seconds.

Pour batter into a 5-inch square cake pan and bake until the cake is springy to the touch, about 30 minutes.

Allow to cool, then cut into four 2½-inch squares.

SAFFRON SYRUP  In a small saucepan, simmer all ingredients together until mixture becomes thick and syrupy, about 10 minutes. Allow to cool, then remove and discard the vanilla pod.

1½ cups flour

1 Tbsp baking powder

1 tsp powdered ginger

½ tsp cinnamon

½ tsp salt

½ cup unsalted butter

¼ cup brown sugar

⅔ cup sugar

1 egg

SAFFRON SYRUP

⅓ cup orange juice

⅓ cup sugar

Pinch of saffron

½ vanilla bean, split and
scraped, but pod reserved

Juice of ½ lemon

SPICED TUILES

1 cup flour

½ tsp cinnamon

½ tsp powdered ginger

¼ tsp grated nutmeg

½ cup unsalted butter

1 cup sugar

½ cup egg whites
(about 4 large eggs)

1 tsp vanilla extract

SPICED TUILES  Preheat the oven to 350°F and line a baking sheet with
a silicone mat or parchment paper.

Sift together flour, cinnamon, ginger and nutmeg.

In the bowl of an electric mixer, cream together butter and sugar using
the paddle attachment until the mixture is fluffy and pale in colour. Gradually add egg whites and vanilla, occasionally scraping the sides of the bowl
to make sure that the ingredients are fully incorporated. Add dry ingredients
while continuing to mix, then scrape the sides of the bowl again.

Using an offset spatula and a 3¾-inch × 1¼-inch rectangular template,
spread a thin layer of batter across the template onto the baking sheet.
Remove the template to leave a rectangle of batter. Repeat until you have
made sixteen tuiles.

Bake in the oven for 5 minutes or until golden brown.

TO SERVE  On each of four plates, place a ginger cake in the middle and top
with a panna cotta. Prop tuiles against each of the four the sides of the cake.
Drizzle syrup on each plate around the cake and garnish with a quarter of
the candied ginger.

SUGGESTED WINE  The rich vanilla and Christmas-pudding flavours of an
Australian liqueur muscat or tokay (actually made from the Bordeaux grape
variety muscadelle) complement the flavours of both the pumpkin and the
ginger cake while standing up to the sweetness of the orange syrup. And
saffron likes oxidative (aged) wine.

# passion fruit soufflé with
# white chocolate crème anglaise

**WHITE CHOCOLATE CRÈME ANGLAISE**

1 cup whole milk

¼ vanilla bean, split and scraped, both seeds and pod reserved

¼ cup sugar

3 egg yolks

2½ oz chopped white chocolate

**PASSION FRUIT SOUFFLÉ**

6 passion fruits

¼ cup granulated sugar

¼ vanilla bean, split and scraped, both seeds and pod reserved

1 tsp cornstarch

½ cup egg whites (about 3 or 4 eggs)

¼ cup icing sugar for dusting

*Serves 4*

WHITE CHOCOLATE CRÈME ANGLAISE   In a medium saucepan, combine milk and vanilla seeds and pod. Bring to a boil.

Meanwhile, whisk together sugar and egg yolks in a medium heatproof mixing bowl until the mixture turns a pale yellow. Slowly add hot milk, whisking constantly. Return this custard to the saucepan and cook on high heat, stirring constantly, until the mixture coats the back of a spoon. Remove and discard the vanilla pod. Pour the custard into a large heatproof mixing bowl. Add white chocolate and whisk to combine.

Cool over an ice bath, then transfer to a creamer until ready to serve.

PASSION FRUIT SOUFFLÉ   Cut passion fruits in half and scrape pulp out into a small saucepan. Whisk in 2 Tbsp of the granulated sugar, vanilla seeds and pod and cornstarch. Bring this mixture to a boil and cook until it thickens, about 5 minutes. Remove from heat and allow to cool.

Grease four ramekins and chill in the freezer for about 10 minutes. Preheat the oven to 350°F.

In the bowl of an electric mixer, beat egg whites until frothy. Add the remaining 2 Tbsp of granulated sugar and continue beating until stiff peaks form. Add passion fruit mixture and beat until stiff peaks form again.

Spoon soufflé mix into ramekins. Tap ramekins to remove air bubbles. Bake for about 10 minutes until golden brown and soufflé has doubled in volume.

TO SERVE   Place a soufflé on each of four plates and dust the top with icing sugar. At the table, wait until your guest has punctured the top of the soufflé with a spoon, then pour a quarter of the crème anglaise overtop.

SUGGESTED WINE   Try Austrian botrytis-affected chardonnay. Its tropical fruit flavours will complement the passion fruit in the soufflé.

# chocolate cappuccino cake
# with mocha espuma

CAKE WITH ESPRESSO
WHIPPED CREAM

13 oz dark chocolate

¼ cup espresso, freshly made

6 eggs, separated

½ cup + 2 Tbsp granulated sugar

1¼ cup whipping cream

¼ cup icing sugar

2 tsp coffee extract

2 tsp cinnamon

CHOCOLATE TUILES

½ cup flour

½ cup cocoa powder

½ cup unsalted butter

1 cup sugar

¾ cup egg whites
(about 6 large eggs)

2 oz dark chocolate, melted in
a microwave to make ¼ cup

MOCHA ESPUMA

2 gelatin leaves, softened
in a little cold water

1½ cups 1% milk

¼ cup sugar

4 tsp espresso

*Serves 6*

To make this cake you'll need coffee extract: add just enough water to instant coffee crystals to make a thick, syrupy mixture. If you don't have a whipped cream dispenser to make the espuma, just garnish the dessert with extra espresso whipped cream.

CAKE  Line a 10-inch square cake pan with parchment paper and preheat the oven to 350°F. In a large heatproof mixing bowl, combine 6 oz of the chocolate and the hot espresso, stirring to melt the chocolate.

In a stainless-steel bowl over a pot of gently simmering water, whisk egg yolks with ¼ cup of the granulated sugar until the mixture is thick and frothy.

In another bowl, whisk egg whites with ¼ cup of the granulated sugar to stiff peaks. Fold egg yolks into the warm chocolate, then fold in egg whites. Pour this batter into the cake pan and bake until dry on top and slightly springy to the touch, about 20 minutes. Remove from the oven and allow to cool. Cut eighteen rounds with a 2-inch cutter.

With an electric mixer, whisk together cream, icing sugar and coffee extract to stiff peaks.

Place a cake round in a 2-inch ring mould. Pipe a layer of whipped cream on top of the cake to cover. Top with another cake round, followed by another layer of whipped cream, then finish with a final cake round. Repeat this process until you have made six cakes, each with three cake rounds. Chill in the refrigerator for about 1 hour, then unmould the cakes.

Cut six 7-inch × 1¾-inch sheets of parchment paper. In a stainless-steel bowl over a pot of simmering water, melt the remaining 7 oz of chocolate.

Spread a wafer-thin layer of chocolate on each sheet of parchment. Lay the sheets out on a baking sheet and chill in the refrigerator until chocolate is solid but still flexible, about 5 minutes. Wrap a chocolate sheet around the side of each cake, then remove and discard the parchment.
*Recipe continued overleaf...*

In a small bowl, combine cinnamon and the remaining 2 Tbsp of granulated sugar and reserve this mixture for garnish.

CHOCOLATE TUILES  Sift together flour and cocoa powder. In the bowl of an electric mixer with a paddle attachment, cream together butter and sugar until the mixture is light and fluffy. Add egg whites gradually, while continuing to mix. Scrape down the sides of the bowl.

Add dry ingredients, then scrape down the sides of the bowl again. Add melted chocolate, then scrape down the bowl and mix for another 10 seconds.

Preheat the oven to 350°F. Line a baking sheet with a silicone mat or parchment paper. Spread tuile batter onto the baking sheet using a template that looks like the side profile of a small cappuccino cup. Repeat until you have made six tuiles. Bake for about 6 minutes, then allow to cool.

MOCHA ESPUMA  Wring the gelatin to remove excess moisture, then combine with ½ cup of the milk in a small saucepan. Gently heat on medium heat until gelatin is dissolved and milk is just scalded, about 5 minutes. Add the remaining 1 cup of milk, sugar and espresso, and mix well. Chill in the refrigerator for about 1 hour. Pour the mixture into a whipped cream dispenser loaded with two nitrous oxide cartridges and keep refrigerated until ready to use.

TO SERVE  In the middle of each of six plates, place a cake. Hang the tuile on the edge of the chocolate sheet so that the sheet resembles a cup and the tuile its handle. Add a dollop of espuma on top and dust with cinnamon sugar. If using espresso whipped cream instead of espuma, pipe a rosette of whipped cream on the cake using a star tip, then dust with cinnamon sugar.

SUGGESTED WINE  The unique soft, mature flavours of a rancio-style banyuls go very well with the chocolate and coffee in this dessert.

# pie

PUMPKIN VODKA

1 small organic sugar
pumpkin, about 4 lbs

1 vanilla bean

1 cinnamon stick

20 cloves

16 pods cardamom

1 bottle vodka (40 oz)

PIE COCKTAIL

1 slice orange, for moistening
the rim of the glass

3 ginger snap cookies,
ground into crumbs

2 oz pumpkin vodka

½ oz simple syrup (page 235)

3½ oz whipping cream,
freshly whipped

Pinch of freshly grated nutmeg

This cocktail smells and tastes just like pumpkin pie with a hit of alcohol. The whipped cream helps to add texture and also hold the nutmeg so that the initial nose carries the freshly grated nut to the senses. Since the alcohol helps preserve the pumpkin infusion indefinitely, prepare plenty of the infusion when pumpkins are in season and store it in the refrigerator so that you always have some at the ready.

PUMPKIN VODKA  Cut pumpkin in half. Remove the pulp and seeds. With a sharp knife, cut the pumpkin into long strips about ¾ inch wide, cut away the skin, then cut the pumpkin flesh into slices ⅛ inch thick.

Place half of the sliced pumpkin into an 8-cup jar with a lid. Slit the vanilla bean lengthwise, then add to the jar. Add cinnamon stick, cloves and cardamom.

Separate the pumpkin pulp from the seeds and put the pulp into the infusion jar. Discard the seeds or reserve them for another recipe. Add the remaining slices of pumpkin and fill the jar with your favourite vodka.

Cover the jar and let it sit for 3 to 4 weeks at room temperature; gently stir the mixture with a spoon every 2 or 3 days.

Line a colander with a single layer of cheesecloth and place it in a large bowl. Pour the pumpkin infusion through the cheesecloth and strain, pressing the pumpkin with a muddling stick or the back of a spoon to extract all the liquid.

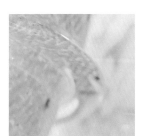

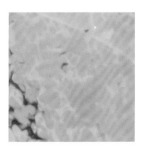

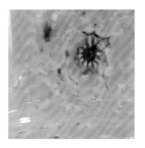

Strain the vodka once again through a new cheesecloth to remove some of the sediment.

Funnel the infused vodka back into an empty bottle and store in the refrigerator until needed.

PIE COCKTAIL Moisten the outer rim of a chilled martini glass with the slice of orange and gently press the glass upside down into the cookie crumbs to coat the rim. Lift the glass straight up, and remove any crumbs from the inside rim with a napkin to prevent crumbs from falling into the cocktail.

Fill a mixing glass with ice and add pumpkin vodka and simple syrup. Shake vigorously until the mixing glass is cold to the touch. If necessary, adjust the balance of sweetness with additional syrup. Strain into the prepared martini glass. Top with a dollop of whipped cream and a dusting of nutmeg.

# hot scott mcdavid

1 slice ginger, dime-thick and
approximately 1 inch in diameter

2 tsp brown sugar

2 cloves

2 wedges of lemon

8 oz boiling water

1½ oz Famous Grouse or other Scotch

1 tsp unsalted butter

Hot cocktails have a great ability to warm us up on cold-weather days, providing comfort and relaxation. This cocktail features flavours that bring memories of Christmas and hot buttered rum, adding a twist with the spice of ginger, savoury taste of clove and a light addition of smoke from the Scotch. Its buttery flavour comes from actual butter, which serves as the garnish. The drink should be stirred before each sip to ensure that the smooth texture and flavour carries through to the end of the drink.

PLACE ginger, sugar, 1 clove and lemon wedges into a mixing glass and muddle well. Add 3 oz of boiling water and allow to sit for about 3 minutes. Strain the infused water through a tea strainer into a heated tea or coffee cup. Add Scotch and top with boiling water. If necessary, adjust the balance of sweetness and acidity to taste with additional sugar or a squeeze of fresh lemon juice. Finish the drink with the butter and remaining clove, then stir and serve.

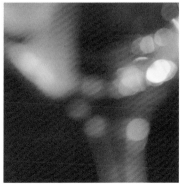

# sora no sato

1 oz Shochu

1 oz Giffard Ginger of the Indies

4 drops freshly squeezed lemon juice

1 piece lemon zest, 2 inches long
and ¼ inch wide, pith removed

Sometimes it doesn't take a lot of ingredients or a massive preparation list to have a cocktail stand out and be noticed. This one captures grace through quiet expression and is light, fresh and crisp, with beautiful notes of ginger. Sora no Sato roughly translates to "Heaven's sugar" in Japanese and uses Shochu, a low-alcohol vodka made with barley, sweet potato or shiso leaves.

PLACE Shochu, ginger liqueur and lemon juice into a mixing glass and half-fill with ice. Stir gently until the mixing glass is cold to the touch. Strain into a chilled martini glass.

Twist lemon zest over the surface of the cocktail to release the citrus oils, then drop it into the glass for garnish.

# before you go—dessert?

Thierry Busset came to the conclusion, after a year at Ouest, that he wanted to work in a bigger restaurant with more seats so that he could, as he puts it, "Be in the action all the time. I enjoy having many people taste my food." He told Jack Evrensel, who was happy to place him at CinCin. As Jack says, "I think Thierry brought that three-star approach to CinCin, and it was infectious." After a brief transition period, Rhonda Viani took over as pastry chef at West. Rhonda is a focussed, energetic, passionate practitioner of the pastry arts. She maintains a tiny station in the kitchen, where she draws and designs her creations and, remarkably, says, "I never repeat anything. I write the recipes down, but basically I am not interested in doing things over and over again. Every day is a new challenge." Thierry notes that "in Canada, people tend to finish their desserts, if they like them. In London, the plates would usually come back with only one or two bites taken." So Rhonda, like Thierry, always knows if she is pleasing her guests. "For me, it is always about doing something new, something interesting, and I have faith that it will work well in the

restaurant if I am doing my best work." Rhonda, intense and articulate, continues: "Sometimes, I am surprised that a dish does not seem to work with the clients. And sometimes, a dish is popular beyond any expectation I have. It is flattering, but then the dessert becomes difficult to remove from the menu, which eventually I need to do." She spends a great deal of time experimenting, trying different things, and agrees fundamentally with Thierry, who says, "Simplicity is key—three to five elements on the plate—and taste is more important than presentation."

The team at West bakes bread and makes the sorbets and ice creams fresh daily, and they make the desserts from scratch each day. Rhonda says, "I always need something about chocolate on the menu. It seems we can never get away without chocolate. But, for me, even though there are seasonal elements, certain fresh fruits for example, I like to try new combinations all the time." So in winter she creates a magnificent saffron-spiced pumpkin panna cotta with ginger cake and orange saffron syrup. One season earlier, in autumn, Rhonda's imagination brings fruit and a bit of sugar together with an herb—a technique she enjoys experimenting with—to invent a sour cream cake with blood orange sorbet and fennel bulb sauce.

Desserts are in some ways the most complete luxury of a fine meal. By the time guests are contemplating dessert, they are already pleasantly satiated and, in many cases, not needing a sugar fix at all. Still, in the hands of an artist such as Rhonda, flavours and textures take on a new dimension, and a fine dessert makes a perfect coda for a fine-dining experience. "I am learning something new every day and trying to make desserts that people will enjoy, while at the same time not simply repeating myself or giving them something they already know. In that sense, what I do is similar to what the other chefs do here." And what exactly is that? To promise each client the best ingredients, skill and effort—each day, each meal, each dish. Then, to fulfill that promise.

# basics

## vegetable stock

...............................

4 carrots, peeled and cut into 1-inch pieces

2 onions, diced

1 head celery, cut into 1-inch pieces

2 bulbs fennel, diced

2 cloves garlic, crushed

4 sprigs thyme

2 bay leaves

10 black peppercorns

6 pods star anise

1 Tbsp fennel seeds

1 Tbsp coriander seeds

20 cups cold water

¾ cup white wine

1 lemon, sliced

3 sprigs each fresh parsley,
    chervil, tarragon and dill

*Makes 20 cups*

Use this stock in place of chicken or fish stock for a slightly lighter result. It can be stored in an airtight container for up to 4 days.

IN a large pot, combine carrots, onions, celery, fennel, garlic, thyme, bay leaves, black peppercorns, star anise, fennel seeds, coriander seeds, water and wine. Bring to a simmer and cook for 30 minutes.

Remove from heat and add lemon and any fresh herb trimmings you may have. Cover with plastic wrap until the stock cools. Pour the stock, along with the vegetables, into containers and store until needed.

## vegetable nage

...............................

2 Tbsp extra-virgin olive oil

2 carrots, sliced

1 Spanish onion, cut into eighths

2 ribs celery, sliced

1 bulb fennel, sliced

1 clove garlic, crushed

1 sprig thyme

1 bay leaf

1 tsp pink peppercorns

2 cups fish stock (page 229)

2 cups water

⅓ cup white wine

⅓ cup white wine vinegar

1 sprig tarragon

1 lemon, sliced

*Makes 4½ cups*

This nage is a bit deeper and richer than the vegetable stock because the vegetables are sautéed first and fish stock is used as a base. It will keep, refrigerated in an airtight container, for up to 3 days.

HEAT olive oil in a large sauté pan on medium heat. Add carrot, onion, celery, fennel, garlic, thyme and bay leaf and sauté until vegetables are soft but not browned, about 15 minutes. Add pink peppercorns, fish stock, water, wine and vinegar. Simmer for 30 minutes.

Remove from heat, then add tarragon and lemon. Allow the nage to cool, then refrigerate until needed.

## court bouillon
............................

20 cups water

1 carrot, roughly chopped

4 ribs celery, halved

1 leek, white part only, quartered

½ medium onion, quartered

2 cloves garlic, crushed

4 tsp white peppercorns

1 Tbsp salt

1 cup white wine

¼ cup white wine vinegar

*Makes 20 cups*

Court bouillon is less densely flavoured than vegetable nage and is slightly acidulated. It is perfect for poaching shellfish.

COMBINE all ingredients in a large stock pot. Bring to a boil and cook for 20 minutes. Remove from heat and allow to stand for 20 minutes. Strain the liquid through a sieve and discard the solids. Refrigerate the court bouillon until needed.

## fish stock
..................

2 lbs fish bones

1 leek, white part only, sliced

½ rib celery, finely chopped

½ onion, finely chopped

¼ bulb fennel, finely chopped

2 cloves garlic, crushed

1 sprig thyme

1 bay leaf

⅓ cup white wine

8 cups cold water

10 white peppercorns, crushed

½ lemon, sliced

2 sprigs parsley

*Makes 8 cups*

This fish stock serves as a base for fish sauces and can be used to poach seafood. Use bones from a white fish; halibut works best. The stock can be stored in an airtight container, refrigerated, for about 2 days, or it can be frozen for future use.

WASH the fish bones for 5 minutes under cold running water. In a large stock pot, combine fish bones, leek, celery, onion, fennel, garlic, thyme and bay leaf. Cover with wine and water and bring to a simmer. Skim the impurities off the surface and add white peppercorns. Simmer for 20 minutes, skimming the surface every 5 minutes or so. Add lemon and parsley, remove from heat and allow to cool. Strain the stock through a fine sieve.

## smoked salmon stock

2 lbs smoked salmon trimmings

1 leek, white part only, sliced

½ rib celery, finely chopped

½ onion, finely chopped

¼ bulb fennel, finely chopped

2 cloves garlic, crushed

1 sprig thyme

1 bay leaf

⅓ cup white wine

8 cups cold water

10 white peppercorns, crushed

½ lemon, sliced

2 sprigs parsley

*Makes 8 cups*

This stock is identical to the fish stock except that it calls for smoked salmon trimmings rather than bones of a white fish, and hence it carries the salmon's smoky flavour. The stock can be stored in an airtight container, refrigerated, for about 3 days, or it can be frozen for up to 1 month.

IN a large stock pot, combine salmon trimmings, leek, celery, onion, fennel, garlic, thyme and bay leaf. Cover with wine and water and bring to a simmer. Skim the impurities off the surface and add white peppercorns. Simmer for 20 minutes, skimming the surface every 5 minutes or so. Add lemon and parsley, remove from heat and allow to cool. Strain the stock through a fine sieve.

## fish velouté

1 Tbsp unsalted butter

6 shallots, finely sliced

10 button mushrooms, finely sliced

1 leek, white part only, finely sliced

1 cup Noilly Prat

4 cups fish stock (page 229)

2 cups whipping cream

*Makes 2 cups*

This velouté is a versatile sauce for seafood-based dishes.

HEAT butter in a large saucepan on medium heat. Add shallots, mushrooms and leek and sweat for 4 to 5 minutes, until soft but not browned. Deglaze the pan with Noilly Prat, then add stock and simmer until the liquid is reduced by two-thirds, about 20 minutes. Add cream and simmer until liquid is reduced by half, about 15 minutes. Pass through a fine sieve.

## shellfish bisque
..............................

5 tsp olive oil

2 lbs shellfish (e.g., crab, lobster, prawn, etc.)
 shells, broken into 1–2-inch pieces

2 ribs celery, chopped

1 carrot, chopped

½ onion, chopped

½ bulb fennel, chopped

1 clove garlic, chopped

2 tsp tomato paste

⅓ cup brandy

6 cups water

1 sprig thyme

⅓ oz tarragon (about 2 tsp)

*Makes 4 cups*

IN a large, heavy-bottomed pan, heat olive oil on high heat. Add shellfish shells and roast for 8 to 10 minutes. Add celery, carrot, onion, fennel and garlic and continue to cook for 6 to 8 minutes. Stir in tomato paste, then add brandy and ignite with a flame to flambé. Once the flame has died down, add water, thyme and tarragon. Bring to a boil, then simmer for 45 minutes, skimming impurities off the surface about once every 10 minutes. Strain the bisque through a cheesecloth and discard the solids.

## lobster essence
..............................

4 cups lobster bisque (shellfish bisque
 made exclusively with lobster shells)

*Makes ¾ cup*

HEAT lobster bisque in a medium pot on medium heat and allow to reduce by 80 per cent, about 25 minutes.

## chicken stock
..............................

4 lbs chicken bones

16 cups cold water

2 ribs celery, coarsely chopped

½ onion, coarsely chopped

2 carrots, coarsely chopped

1 sprig thyme

1 bay leaf

*Makes 8 cups*

Chicken stock is one of the most versatile and widely used bases for all sorts of soups and sauces. This stock can be stored in an airtight container in the fridge for 2 days or frozen for up to 1 month.

IN a large stock pot, cover bones with 8 cups of the cold water. Bring to a boil, then remove from heat and strain the bones in a sieve to remove excess protein. Return the bones to the pan and cover with the remaining 8 cups of water. Add celery, onion, carrots, thyme and bay leaf and bring this mixture to a boil, then allow to simmer for 90 minutes. Strain the liquid through a cheesecloth.

## chicken velouté

......................................

1 Tbsp unsalted butter

6 shallots, peeled and thinly sliced

2 cups white wine

4 cups chicken stock (page 231)

2 cups whipping cream

*Makes 5 cups*

Chicken velouté can serve as a handy sauce for chicken dishes. It can be stored in an airtight container in the refrigerator for up to 3 days.

IN a large saucepan, heat butter on medium heat. Add shallots and sauté for 3 to 4 minutes, until soft but not browned. Deglaze the pan with wine. Add chicken stock and continue to cook until liquid is reduced by half, about 15 minutes. Add cream. Simmer 5 minutes, then strain through a fine sieve.

## roasting jus

......................

¼ cup olive oil

6 chicken legs, chopped as finely as possible

1¼ cups water

1¼ cups chicken stock (page 231)

1¼ cups brown veal and chicken jus (page 232)

*Makes 2 cups*

This basic brown sauce can be stored in the refrigerator for up to 3 days.

PREHEAT the oven to 400°F. Add olive oil to a hot roasting pan and add chicken legs. Place the pan in the oven and roast until chicken is golden brown, about 1 hour.

Remove from the oven and cover with the water, stock and jus. Simmer on medium-low for 1 hour. Strain the liquid through a fine sieve into a medium saucepan, pressing the bones to extract all of the liquid.

On medium heat, simmer liquid for 15 to 20 minutes until it is reduced by half.

## brown veal and chicken jus

..............................................

4 lbs veal bones

4 lbs chicken bones

10 cups water or enough to cover bones

6 ribs celery, roughly chopped

3 carrots, roughly chopped

1 large onion, roughly chopped

2 leeks, white parts only, roughly chopped

2 cloves garlic

3 sprigs thyme

*Makes 4 cups*

PREHEAT the oven to 350°F. Place bones in a large roasting pan and roast in the oven for 30 to 40 minutes until golden brown. Transfer the bones to a large pot, add enough water to cover and bring to a boil, skimming any impurities off the surface. Add celery, carrots, onion, leeks, garlic and thyme and simmer for 2 to 3 hours. Strain the jus through a cheesecloth into a medium saucepan and discard the solids. Heat the saucepan on medium heat until the liquid has reduced by two-thirds, about 45 minutes.

## red wine jus

.....................

2 cups red wine

1⅓ cups ruby port

4 shallots, sliced

1 sprig thyme

2 cups brown veal and chicken jus (page 232)

*Makes 1 cup*

Use this jus as a rich and intensely flavoured sauce for roasted red meats. It can be stored in an airtight container in the refrigerator for 3 to 4 days or frozen for 2 months.

IN a medium saucepan, heat red wine, ruby port, shallots and thyme until liquid has reduced by three-quarters, about 25 minutes. Add jus, bring to a boil, then simmer for 12 to 15 minutes until reduced by one-third.

## chicken mousse

.....................

7 oz chicken breast

½ tsp kosher salt

Pinch of white pepper

1 egg white

1 cup whipping cream

*Makes 2 cups*

This mousse can be used as a binding agent for ravioli fillings. It can be stored no more than 2 days, refrigerated, in an airtight container.

IN a food processor, purée chicken breast until smooth, then season with salt and white pepper. Add egg white while continuing to mix, then slowly add ½ cup of the cream.

Pass this mixture through a fine sieve into a bowl set over ice. Fold in remaining cream 1 Tbsp at a time.

## salmon mousse

.....................

7 oz fresh salmon

½ tsp kosher salt

Pinch of white pepper

1 egg white

1 cup whipping cream

*Makes 2 cups*

This salmon mousse is simlar to the chicken mousse but can be used for seafood-based dishes.

IN a food processor, purée salmon until smooth, then season with salt and white pepper. Add egg white while continuing to mix, then slowly add ½ cup of the cream.

Pass this mixture through a fine sieve into a bowl set over ice. Fold in remaining cream 1 Tbsp at a time.

## clarified butter

1 cup unsalted butter

*Makes ⅔ cup*

Clarified butter is simply butter from which the milk solids have been removed and hence can be heated to high temperatures without burning.

IN a small, heavy-bottomed saucepan, melt butter on medium heat, then boil it gently for 5 minutes. Remove it from the heat and allow it to settle for about 10 minutes. Skim the foam off the surface of the butter, then pour the clarified butter into a jar, leaving the milk solids at the bottom of the pan. Allow the clarified butter to cool, then cover with a tight-fitting lid and refrigerate.

## curry butter

½ tsp turmeric

½ tsp coriander seeds

¼ tsp powdered ginger

¼ tsp cumin

2 cardamom pods

¼ tsp mace

½ tsp fennel seeds

½ tsp caraway seeds

Pinch of cayenne pepper

1 clove

1⅓ cups unsalted butter, softened to room temperature

*Makes 1⅓ cups*

IN a spice grinder or using a mortar and pestle, grind together turmeric, coriander seeds, ginger, cumin, cardamom, mace, fennel seeds, caraway seeds, cayenne and clove to a powder. Sift through a sieve, then fold the spice powder into butter.

## acid butter

....................

¾ cup white wine

½ cup white wine vinegar

1 onion, chopped

¾ cup unsalted butter

*Makes 2 cups*

Acid butter can be used to finish a risotto; the acidity helps to cleanse the palate.

IN a small saucepan, combine wine, vinegar and onion and cook on medium heat until reduced to a syrup, about 20 minutes. Add butter, stir until melted, pass through a fine sieve and chill in the refrigerator, stirring every 10 to 15 minutes until set.

## simple syrup

....................

2 cups sugar

2 cups water

*Makes 2 cups*

This simple syrup should not be confused with sugar syrup, which is used in dessert recipes.

IN a small saucepan, mix sugar and water. Bring to a slow simmer, stirring to make sure all of the sugar dissolves. Simmer the syrup for 1 minute after it boils. Allow to cool.

## sugar syrup

....................

1 cup sugar

¾ cup water

¼ cup corn syrup

*Makes 1 cup*

This sugar syrup is used in dessert recipes and should not be confused with simple syrup.

IN a small saucepan mix sugar, water and corn syrup and bring to a simmer for 5 minutes. Allow to cool.

## candied walnuts

....................

12 oz walnut wholes or halves, shelled

⅔ cup icing sugar

8 cups vegetable oil for deep frying

*Makes 1 lb*

This recipe works well with most nuts and is very versatile. Use the walnuts with cheese or in a salad or simply eat them on their own.

PLACE walnuts in a pot and cover with water. Simmer for 3 minutes, drain and allow to cool. Pour icing sugar overtop and thoroughly mix.

In a deep fryer or a deep pot, heat vegetable oil to 350°F. Add walnuts and fry until crisp, 2 to 3 minutes, then drain and lightly salt. Keep in an airtight container.

## lemon reduction

.....................................

Juice of 2 lemons

*Makes 2 tsp*
This reduction adds an intense lemon flavour to a host of desserts. Use immediately after making.

IN a small saucepan, simmer lemon juice on medium heat until it is reduced to the consistency of honey, about 8 minutes. Remove from heat and allow to cool.

## citrus dressing

.....................................

Zest of 1 lemon
Juice of 2 lemons
⅓ cup extra-virgin olive oil
1 Tbsp sugar

*Makes ½ cup*
This versatile dressing matches with almost any type of salad green and also works well with seafood.

WHISK all ingredients together until sugar is dissolved and add kosher salt and freshly ground white pepper to taste.

## sherry dressing

.....................................

1 cup sherry vinegar
2 Tbsp Dijon mustard
2½ cups light olive oil

*Makes 3½ cups*
This dressing is great for salad greens accompanying a dish of cured meat.

IN a medium bowl, whisk together vinegar and mustard and season with salt and pepper. Add oil in a thin stream while continuing to whisk until the dressing is emulsified.

## pasta dough

......................

1⅓ lbs Italian 00 flour (about 5 cups)

4 eggs

6 egg yolks

1 tsp salt

1 oz extra-virgin olive oil

*Makes 1½ lbs*

This recipe can be used for any variety of pasta, including ravioli, tortellini, cannelloni, fettuccine and lasagna. This recipe calls for Italian 00 flour, which is highly refined and soft. It is available at Italian and specialty food stores, but if you cannot find it, use a high-quality semolina flour. The quantity called for is very precise, so weigh the flour if you can.

PLACE the flour in a food processor and pulse the machine a few times while slowly adding eggs and egg yolks. Add salt and oil and mix continuously until everything has come together.

Remove the dough from the machine and knead for about 10 minutes, until the pasta feels smooth.

Tightly wrap the dough in plastic wrap. Allow to rest for at least 2 hours.

## tomatoes concassé

......................

10 ripe Roma tomatoes

*Makes 10 tomatoes*

Tomatoes concassé simply refers to tomatoes that have been peeled, deseeded and diced. Blanching the tomatoes allows their skin to be easily removed. They are best prepared fresh, but if you have leftovers, store them in the refrigerator in an airtight container.

BRING a large pot of water to a boil. Add tomatoes and blanch for 10 seconds. Remove and discard the skin and seeds and coarsely dice the tomato.

## deep-fried parsley

......................

1 cup vegetable oil for deep frying

1 sprig parsley, leaves picked off and stem discarded

*Makes 1 sprig*

Parsley is already a ubiquitous garnish, but deep frying the herb first makes it completely edible rather than leaving stringy pieces in your mouth. You can apply this same technique to any green leafy herb.

HEAT a deep-fryer or a deep pot of vegetable oil to 400°F. Plunge in parsley leaves and fry for 4 to 5 seconds. Remove the parsley from the oil, drain on paper towels and season lightly with salt.

## basil oil

......................

3½ oz basil

⅓ cup olive oil

*Makes ⅓ cup*

This beautiful oil is incredibly fragrant and also adds great colour. Other soft-leaved herbs can be treated the same way.

BRING a small pot of water to a boil. Add basil and blanch for 15 seconds, then plunge the basil into an ice bath to refresh. Wring out any excess moisture from the basil and place it in a blender. Season with salt and pepper, then add oil and blend for 2 to 3 minutes. Pass the oil through a fine sieve.

## duck confit

......................

8 duck legs

⅓ cup coarse salt

1 Tbsp black peppercorns, crushed

1 clove garlic, sliced

1 sprig thyme

1 bay leaf, crumbled

Zest of ½ orange

4 cups duck fat, warmed

10 round shallots

3 Tbsp sherry vinegar

*Makes 8 duck legs*

To confit something typically means to cook slowly in fat or oil. The process yields a tender, flavourful and moist product. Duck confit is cooked in duck fat, which is available at most specialty food stores. Leftover duck confit should be stored in the fat and refrigerated.

IN a bowl, rub duck legs with coarse salt, black peppercorns, garlic, thyme, bay leaf and orange zest. Cover with plastic wrap and refrigerate for 16 hours.

Rinse the rub off the duck legs and place them in a pot. Cover with duck fat. Bring to 175°F and cook for approximately 2½ hours, or until the meat is tender and falls off the bone. One hour into cooking the duck, add shallots.

Remove the shallots and duck legs from the fat. Pull the meat off the duck legs, discarding the bones and skin. In a medium bowl, mix the shallots and duck meat together. Season with salt, pepper and sherry vinegar. Add 1 Tbsp of the duck fat to keep the duck moist.

## pickling liquor

. . . . . . . . . . . . . . . . . . . . . . . . . . .

Pinch of cracked white pepper

½ tsp coriander seeds

½ tsp mace

1 pod star anise

4 pods cardamom

1½ tsp cumin seeds

¾ cup cider vinegar

1½ cups white wine vinegar

1¼ cups Sauternes

1 cup sugar

3 cups olive oil

*Makes 6 cups*

COMBINE all ingredients in a large saucepan and heat on low heat to 175°F, measuring the temperature with a thermometer. Allow to cool, then strain through a sieve, reserving the liquid and discarding the solids.

## mayonnaise

. . . . . . . . . . . . . . . . . . . . . .

1 egg

2 tsp Dijon mustard

3½ Tbsp white wine vinegar

2 cups vegetable oil

*Makes 2 cups*

COMBINE egg, mustard and vinegar in a blender. When the mixture is thoroughly blended, slowly add oil in a thin stream while continuing to mix, to form an emulsion. If the mayonnaise is too thick, add a little cold water. Season with salt and pepper.

# conversion charts

## weight
(rounded to nearest even whole number)

| IMPERIAL | METRIC |
| --- | --- |
| 1 oz | 28 g |
| 2 oz | 58 g |
| 3 oz | 86 g |
| 4 oz | 114 g |
| 5 oz | 142 g |
| 6 oz | 170 g |
| 7 oz | 198 g |
| 8 oz (½ lb) | 226 g |
| 9 oz | 256 g |
| 10 oz | 284 g |
| 11 oz | 312 g |
| 12 oz | 340 g |
| 13 oz | 368 g |
| 14 oz | 396 g |
| 15 oz | 426 g |
| 16 oz (1 lb) | 454 g |

## volume
(rounded to closest equivalent)

| IMPERIAL | METRIC |
| --- | --- |
| ⅛ tsp | 0.5 mL |
| ¼ tsp | 1 mL |
| ½ tsp | 2.5 mL |
| ¾ tsp | 4 mL |
| 1 tsp | 5 mL |
| 1 Tbsp | 15 mL |
| 1½ Tbsp | 25 mL |
| ⅛ cup | 30 mL |
| ¼ cup | 60 mL |
| ⅓ cup | 80 mL |
| ½ cup | 120 mL |
| ⅔ cup | 160 mL |
| ¾ cup | 180 mL |
| 1 cup | 240 mL |

## liquid
(rounded to closest equivalent)

| IMPERIAL | METRIC |
| --- | --- |
| 1 oz | 30 mL |
| 1½ oz | 45 mL |
| 2 oz | 60 mL |
| 3 oz | 90 mL |
| 4 oz | 120 mL |
| 6 oz | 180 mL |
| 8 oz | 240 mL |

## linear
(rounded to closest equivalent)

| IMPERIAL | METRIC |
| --- | --- |
| ⅛ inch | 3 mm |
| ¼ inch | 6 mm |
| 1 inch | 2.5 cm |
| 1¼ inches | 3 cm |
| 6 inches | 15 cm |
| 8 inches | 20 cm |
| 9 inches | 22.5 cm |

## temperature
(rounded to closest equivalent)

| IMPERIAL | METRIC |
| --- | --- |
| 150°F | 65°C |
| 160°F | 70°C |
| 175°F | 80°C |
| 200°F | 95°C |
| 225°F | 105°C |
| 250°F | 120°C |
| 275°F | 135°C |
| 300°F | 150°C |
| 325°F | 160°C |
| 350°F | 180°C |
| 375°F | 190°C |
| 400°F | 205°C |
| 425°F | 220°C |
| 150°F | 230°C |
| 475°F | 245°C |
| 500°F | 260°C |

# acknowledgements

THANKS ARE DUE to so many for the successful completion of this cookbook. First among them is the dedicated team at West and the very talented people who lead that team: Warren Geraghty, Rhonda Viani, Stephanie Noel, Brian Hopkins, Owen Knowlton, David Wolowidnyk, Corey Bauldry, Erin Evans and Lawrence Fung. Thanks also to alumni for their past contributions: Thierry Busset, Andrew Richardson, Marc-André Choquette, Chris Van Nus and expressly David Hawksworth, who contributed recipes to this book. I would also like to thank Shelley McArthur and Neil Henderson from Top Table and the late Werner Forster for his gift to us all.

This cookbook would not have been possible without the support of the team at Douglas & McIntyre—including Scott McIntyre and Chris Labonté, who championed the project; art director Peter Cocking; designer Jessica Sullivan and editor Iva Cheung—or without John Sherlock, who bore witness with brilliant photography, and Jim Tobler, who relentlessly tried to understand us, pen in hand.

JACK EVRENSEL

# index

DUCK
    broth, 143
    confit, 238
    confit, breasts and consommé,
        204–05
Dungeness crab tortellini with cauli-
    flower purée, pickled florets and
    light crab bisque, 19–20

egg, crispy quail, 132
eggplant and pine nut cannelloni, 97–98
eggplant caviar, 146

fennel bulb sauce, 162
fennel, roasted, 155
figs, Marsala-roasted, 105
fillet of ling cod with roasted fennel
    and ragout of calamari, 154, 155–56
fillet of mackerel with cannelloni
    of smoked eggplant and pine
    nuts, 96, 97–98
FISH
    halibut braised over mushrooms, 95
    halibut, pan-fried, 31
    ling cod, with roasted fennel and
        ragout of calamari, 155–56
    ling cod, with spicy braised pork
        belly, 32–33
    mackerel fillet with cannelloni, 97–98
    salmon, confit, 89
    salmon mousse, 233
    salmon, smoked, gnocchi, 88–89
    salmon, smoked, stock, 230
    salmon supreme, 90–91
    salmon with twelve vegetables, 93
    skate, and crab tian, 15–16
    snapper, Thai, tartare, 80–81
    stock, 229
    sturgeon with velouté of saffron,
        mussels and bacon, 99

tuna, and veal with olive panisse,
    40–41
tuna carpaccio, 126
velouté, 230
FOIE GRAS, 184–85
    and goat cheese and apple
        terrine, 70–71
    parfait, 184
    with rhubarb and cinnamon purée
        and pomme allumettes, 21
frangipane, 103
freestone peaches poached with
    Moscato d'Asti with frangipane
    and blackberry coulis, 103
fresh raspberries with lemon tuiles,
    cream cheese ice cream and nobo
    fruit tea syrup, 106, 107–08
frozen lemon-tamarind soufflé, 46–48

galantine of quail, foie gras and
    jasmine-poached raisins, 184–85
garlic, confit, 125
GARNISH. See also deep-fried herbs
    baby fennel, 153
    blood orange, 163
    chanterelle, 181
gazpacho, smoked tomato, 78
GINGER
    cake, 210–11
    -cilantro gremolata, 127
    ice cream, 52–53
gnocchi, smoked salmon, 90
GOAT CHEESE, 67. See also cheese
    apple and foie gras terrine, 70–71
    with multicoloured beets baked
        on salt, 66
    ravioli, 88–89
    tortellini with artichoke barigoule,
        68–69
    and vine-ripened tomato velouté, 85

grape compote, 164
grapefruit espuma, 207
grapefruit, honey-roasted, 207
green apple and ginger purée, 81
green olive tapenade, 150
gremolata, ginger-cilantro, 127

halibut and chanterelles with
    watercress sauce and lasagna
    of crab, 30–31
halibut braised over mushrooms,
    94, 95
hazelnut praline, 160–61
heirloom tomato water, 113
herb-crusted saddle of new season lamb
    with sweet and sour shallots, 34–35
herbed bread crumbs, 99
HONEY, 208
    and black pepper–roasted duck breast
        with crisp confit and spiced duck
        consommé, 204–05
    coconut ice cream, 43, 45
    -roasted grapefruit, 207
hummus, 13

ICE CREAM. See also sorbet
    apple-rosemary, 160
    coconut honey, 43, 44, 45
    cream cheese, 107
    ginger, 52–53
    vanilla, 104
icewine grape sorbet, 164–65

jasmine green tea syrup, 109
jasmine-poached raisins, 184
JUS
    brown veal and chicken, 232
    quail, 180–81
    red wine, 233
    roasting, 232